FUNDAMENTAL MORAL THEOLOGY

UNITS ONE AND TWO

GW00633779

THE PRIORY INSTITUTE

1

THE PRIORY INSTITUTE

The Priory Institute, established in the Dominican tradition, is a centre for education in theological and biblical studies. It offers an extensive range of seminars and programmes including a certificate, diploma and degree in theology by distance learning in association with the University of Wales, Lampeter, and a part-time degree in theology in association with HETAC and the Institute of Technology, Tallaght.

THE PRIORY INSTITUTE TEAM

Joseph Kavanagh *moderator*
John Littleton *distance education manager*
Martin Cogan *general editor*
Joseph Cullen *adult education director*
Joan Nolan *office administration and accounts*

THEOLOGY FOR TODAY

Level One: (certificate programme)

1. Introduction to Theology
2. Introduction to Scripture
3. Introduction to Philosophy
4. Introduction to Christian Spirituality

Levels Two and Three: (diploma and degree programmes)

5. Fundamental Theology
6. Themes in Modern Philosophy
7. The God of Christian Faith
8. Fundamental Moral Theology
9. Church History
10. Christianity and World Religions
11. The Gospel of Mark
12. A Just Society
13. Isaiah and Biblical Prophecy
14. Philosophical Theology
15. Trinity & Incarnate Word
16. Caring for Life
17. Soteriology and Eschatology
18. The Psalms
19. Church and Sacraments
20. Pauline Writings

FUNDAMENTAL MORAL THEOLOGY

Series:	Theology for Today
Series Number:	Eight
Title:	Fundamental Moral Theology Volume One
Contents:	Unit One: Fundamental Moral Concepts
	Unit Two: Nature, Reason, Law and Growth
ISBN:	1-905193-16-5
Authors:	Charles Bouchard, Archie Byrne, Amelia Flemming, Paul Philibert
Published by:	The Priory Institute
Editors:	Martin Cogan and John Littleton
Typesetting:	The Priory Institute
Design:	Eddie McManus Graphics
Printing:	The Leinster Leader Ltd, Naas, Co Kildare, Ireland

The Priory Institute
Tallaght Village, Dublin 24, Ireland
Telephone: (+353-1) 404 8124. Fax: (+353-1) 462 6084
email: enquiries@prioryinstitute.com   Website: www.prioryinstitute.com

FUNDAMENTAL MORAL THEOLOGY
MODULE CONTENTS

VOLUME ONE: (THIS VOLUME)
UNIT ONE: FUNDAMENTAL MORAL CONCEPTS
UNIT TWO: NATURE, REASON, LAW AND GROWTH

VOLUME TWO: (NEXT VOLUME)
UNIT THREE: THE VIRTUES
UNIT FOUR: CHRISTIAN MORALITY IN CONTEXT

MODULE INTRODUCTION

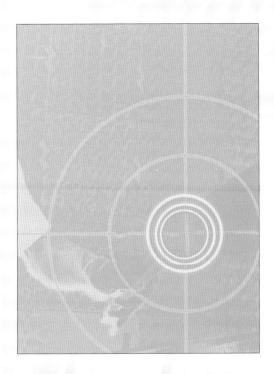

I.   GROWTH IN HAPPINESS, VIRTUE AND GRACE

Questions of morality are all around us, whether explicitly or implicitly. The media constantly confronts us with moral issues on the actions of businesses, nations, individuals and churches. Everyone has some instinct about what is right and wrong, but when pushed to it, how can people really explain the deeper reasons why they believe some actions are right and others wrong.

It may come as a surprise to some, but not all systems of morality examine lists of individual actions and tabulate their moral value. Some systems begin by looking at the overall goal or desire of human life, and only then look to the means whereby a person grows towards the deepest goals. In these approaches to morality, individual moral actions are thought of as contributing (or not) towards the attainment of that goal. This is the more dynamic approach, as distinct from the simpler 'black and white' approach of treating moral actions in isolation.

2.   THE STRUCTURE OF THE MODULE

This module contains fourteen distinct sections, seven in the first volume and seven in the second. The first unit of Volume One begins by asking what it means to be moral, and goes on to outline the major theories of morality in use today, whether Christian or non-Christian. The first unit also explores what is necessary for any individual act to be designated a fully moral action – what is known as 'a human act'. The bulk of this first unit, and of those section which follow in Unit Two contain philosophical thought which can apply to any reasonable human being. There is nothing specifically Christian about much of this material, it can be adopted and discussed by anybody. The material on 'natural law' in Unit Two is based on a trust in human reason's ability to distinguish right from wrong. This rational, natural law theory is at the base of a great deal of Christian and Catholic moral teaching, even though the thinking involved could be understood by anyone, Christian or not. Also in Unit Two, the theories of the experimental psychologists Piaget and Kohlberg are examined, and in their work the development of moral thinking in children and adults is studied.

In Unit Three, the concern is with what are called the 'cardinal virtues'; these are the virtues which govern proper behaviour in any human life. Even though these are examined in a more specifically Christian setting, the original thinking for this unit stems from the Greek philosopher, Aristotle (384-322 bce), and has been utilised extensively by Christian theologians such as Augustine (354-430 ce) and, especially, Aquinas (1225-1274 ce).

Only in Unit Four does the module concentrate more exclusively on Christian teaching, drawn partly on the scriptures. Unit Four examines what makes a morality specifically Christian, and asks what role does grace have in the moral life, and where does the Spirit enter situations and circumstances? The final section of Unit Four then takes a very speculative view of life in the Church, and sees how one can live in the Church with various levels of hope and trust in God's grace.

3. LEARNING OUTCOMES

By the end of this module, the student should have a good understanding of:

a)   the main philosophical schools of moral thought;

b)   the kernel of human moral actions – the 'human act' – and the requirements for any action to be considered fully human;

c)   the steps a person goes through in making one, single, moral act;

d)   the concept of 'autonomy' on the path to moral maturity;

e)   the role which law plays in different moral philosophies; as well as what it means to break the law, and how such breakages relate to moral decline or growth;

f)   the importance of reason in morality, and the idea of 'natural law' in particular;

g)   the contribution of twentieth-century thinkers, Jean Piaget and Lawrence Kohlberg, to the understanding of the development of moral thinking in children, from childhood to adulthood;

h)   the function of virtue in the moral life, and the role played by the theological virtues of faith, hope and charity, and the cardinal virtues of prudence, justice, courage (fortitude) and moderation (temperance);

i)   moral living within the Church – the communal nature of morality.

CONTENTS

FUNDAMENTAL MORAL THEOLOGY

UNITS ONE AND TWO

	MODULE INTRODUCTION	V
1.	GROWTH IN HAPPINESS, VIRTUE AND GRACE	V
2.	THE STRUCTURE OF THE MODULE	V
3.	LEARNING OUTCOMES	VI

UNIT ONE FUNDAMENTAL MORAL CONCEPTS

	INTRODUCTION TO UNIT ONE	3
1.	KNOWLEDGE, PURPOSE AND REASON	3
2.	THE STRUCTURE OF UNIT ONE	3
3.	LEARNING OUTCOMES	4
SECTION ONE:	WHY BE MORAL?	5
1.	MORALITY AND THE WORLD AROUND US	5
1.1	Morality on the World Stage	5
1.2	Morality all Around Us	6
2.	WHAT IS MORAL KNOWING?	6
2.1	The Emotivist Approach	6
2.2	The Intuitive Approach	7
2.3	Emotivist or Intuitive?	7
3.	NORMATIVE APPROACHES TO ETHICS	8
3.1	The Deontological Approach	8
3.2	Civic Legalism	8
3.3	Religious Legalism	8
3.4	Extrinsic Legalism	8
3.5	Formalism	9
3.6	Conventionalism	9
4.	TELEOLOGICAL APPROACHES TO ETHICS	9
4.1	Ethical Egoism	9
4.2	Ethical Hedonism	10
4.3	Utilitarianism	10
4.4	Consequentialism	10
5.	MORALITY AS A SEARCH FOR HAPPINESS	11
5.1	Experience	12
5.2	Reason	13
5.3	Freedom	13
5.4	Vision	13
5.5	Judgment and Action	14
6.	REASON, REVELATION AND MORAL THEOLOGY	14
6.1	Duty or Happiness?	14
6.2	Natural Law	15
7.	THE RELIGIOUS DIMENSION OF FULFILMENT ETHICS	15
7.1	Can One Trust in Reason?	15
7.2	Nature and Grace	16
7.3	The Holy Spirit and the Moral Life	17

SECTION TWO: HUMAN ACTS 18

1. THE BUILDING BLOCKS OF THE MORAL LIFE 18
1.1 Moral Freedom 18
1.2 Knowledge 19
1.3 Emotions 19
1.4 Psychological or Chemical Factors 19
1.5 Two Levels of Freedom 20

2. HUMAN ACTS IN CONTEXT 21
2.1 Useful Traditional Principles 21
2.2 The Three Fonts of Morality 22
    The Act Itself 22
    The Intention 22
    The Circumstances 22
2.3 The Principle of Double Effect 23
2.4 Proportionality 24
2.5 The Principle of Cooperation 25
    Formal and Material Cooperation 25
2.6 Health-Care Ethics 25

3. MORAL AGENCY AND INTRINSIC EVIL 26
3.1 Does Intrinsic Evil Exist? 26
3.2 Proportionalism 27

4. CONSCIENCE AND THE VIRTUE OF PRUDENCE 28
4.1 The Judgement of Conscience 28
4.2 Conscience and Virtue 28
4.3 Habitus 29
4.4 Prudence 29
4.5 Action 30
4.6 Virtues in Art 30

SECTION THREE: STRUCTURE OF MORAL DECISION-MAKING 32

1. THE BASIS OF HUMAN CHOICE 32
1.1 Basic Elements 32
1.2 Human Behaviour 32
1.3 The Interaction of Mind and Will 33

2. PHASE ONE: GOOD INTENTIONS 33
2.1 Assessing What is Possible 33
2.2 Basic Motivation 34

3. PHASE TWO: WAYS AND MEANS 34
3.1 Selecting One Way 34
3.2 From 'Can Do' to 'Should Do' 35

4. PHASE THREE: IMPLEMENTING THE DECISION 35
4.1 Mind and Will Rejoice 35

5. MORALITY IN DECISION MAKING 36
5.1 Values, Aspirations and Convictions 36
5.2 What Must I Do? 36
5.3 Considering All the Options 37
5.4 Areas of Moral Reflection 37
5.5 Assistance in Moral Reflection 38

FUNDAMENTAL MORAL THEOLOGY

6.	THE MOMENT OF TRUTH	38
6.1	What Must I Do?	38
6.2	Basic Inclinations	39
6.3	The Guarantee of Rectitude	39
7.	RESOLVING MORAL DOUBTS	39
7.1	Following the Safer Course	40
7.2	'Final Practical Judgement' and 'Conscience'	40
7.3	Conflicting Values	41
7.4	Competing Moral Values	41
8.	CONCLUSIONS	42
SECTION FOUR:	AUTONOMY AND THEONOMY	43
1.	THE PATH TO MORAL MATURITY	43
2.	AUTONOMY IN MORALS	43
2.1	Autonomy and Theonomy	43
2.2	Grace: New Life, New Morals	44
2.3	Life before Morals	44
2.4	Fatal Attraction/Forbidden Fruit	45
2.5	Is Revolt an Answer?	46
2.6	Is Conformity an Answer?	46
3.	TOWARDS MORAL MATURITY	47
3.1	Growing in Love	47
3.2	Reading the Signs of the Times	48
3.3	The Law of Love	48
4.	VIRTUES: THE ART OF GOOD LIVING	49
4.1	Aquinas on Habit	49
4.2	Theological and Cardinal Virtues	50
4.3	Presiding Virtues	51
4.4	Good Inclinations	51
4.5	Virtues Working Together	51
	CONCLUSIONS TO UNIT ONE	53
1.	FREEDOM AND INDEPENDENCE	53
2.	LEARNING OUTCOMES ASSESSED	54

UNIT TWO: NATURE, REASON, LAW AND GROWTH

		INTRODUCTION TO UNIT TWO	
	1.	LAW AND NATURE, GRACE AND REASON	.57
	2.	THE CONTENT OF UNIT TWO	.57
	3.	LEARNING OUTCOMES	.58
SECTION ONE		MORALITY AND LAW	.59
	1.	FUNDAMENTAL IDEAS ABOUT LAW	.59
	1.1	Troubles with the Idea of Law	.60
	1.2	Aquinas on Law	.61
	2.	AUTONOMY AND HETERONOMY	.61
	2.1	Authenticity and Intimidation	.61
	3.	DESCRIBING LAW	.63
	3.1	Essential Aspects of law	.63
	3.2	Human Necessity	.63
	3.3	The Law of Reason	.63
	3.4	The Common Good	.64
	4.	CANON LAW	.66
	4.1	The Authority of Canon Law	.67
	5.	LAW IN THE SCRIPTURES	.67
	5.1	The Old Testament Use of Law	.67
	5.2	the New Testament Use of Law	.68
	5.3	New Replaces the Old	.68
	6.	THE SOURCE OF ALL LAW	.70
	7.	AUTHORITY AND GRACE	.71
	7.1	Two Versions of Moral Responsibility	.71
	7.2	The Human Personality	.72
	7.3	Ockham's Nominalism	.73
	7.4	Two Concepts of Conscience	.74
SECTION TWO		NATURAL LAW	.76
	1.	HOW WE KNOW MORAL TRUTH	.76
	2.	THE ORIGIN OF NATURAL LAW	.77
	2.1	Scriptural Origins	.77
	2.2	Natural Law History: The Greeks & Romans	.77
	2.3	Natural Law History: The Middle Ages	.78
	2.4	Natural Law from the Heart	.80
	3.	DOES NATURAL LAW CHANGE?	.80
	3.1	Static or Evolving?	.80
	4.	IMPLICATIONS OF NATURAL LAW	.82
	4.1	Sexual Ethics and Natural Law	.82
	4.2	Natural Law and Health-Care	.82
	4.3	Social Ethics	.83
	5.	NATURAL LAW AND REVELATION	.83
	5.1	Open to All	.83
	5.2	Natural Foundation for Grace	.84
	6.	NATURAL LAW AND SPIRITUALITY	.85
	6.1	Life in Society	.85

6.2	Fear of Nature	85
6.3	Trust in Nature	86
SECTION THREE	THE MORAL DEVELOPMENT OF THE HUMAN PERSON	87
1.	TWO ACCOUNTS OF HUMAN DEVELOPMENT	87
2.	HUMANISATION	87
2.1	Søren Kierkegaard	88
2.2	William James	88
2.3	Sigmund Freud	89
3.	PIAGET AND KOHLBERG	89
4.	JEAN PIAGET	90
4.1	Genetic Epistemology	90
4.2	The Development of Human Intelligence	91
	Stage One: Sensorimotor Learning	91
	Stage Two: Pre-Operational Thinking	93
	Stage Three: Interaction	94
	Stage Four: Deductive and Creative Logic	95
4.3	Piaget's Analysis of Moral Thinking	96
	Heteronomy	97
	Autonomy	97
	Co-operation and Social Restraint	97
4.4	Summary	98
5.	THE MORAL SYSTEM OF LAWRENCE KOHLBERG	99
5.1	A Life-Span Framework	99
5.2	Moral Thinking at the Preconventional Level	99
5.3	Moral Thinking at the Conventional Level	100
5.4	The Postconventional or Autonomous Level	101
5.5	Six Stages of Moral Development	102
6.	THE STRUCTURES OF MORAL DEVELOPMENT	102
6.1	Overcoming Ambiguity	102
6.2	Facing Up to Injustice	103
6.3	Broader Understanding	103
1.	CONCLUSIONS TO UNIT TWO	105
2.	LEARNING OUTCOMES ASSESSED	106
	BIBLIOGRAPHY	107
	FURTHER READING	109
	GLOSSARY	110

FUNDAMENTAL MORAL THEOLOGY

PROGRAMME
THEOLOGY FOR TODAY

MODULE
FUNDAMENTAL MORAL THEOLOGY

UNIT ONE

FUNDAMENTAL MORAL CONCEPTS

INTRODUCTION TO UNIT ONE

Morality

1. KNOWLEDGE, PURPOSE AND REASON

This initial unit approaches fundamental moral theory by way of reason and philosophy. The unit examines all the relevant modern and ancient theories of morality in isolation from questions of God or belief. Where does one find one's fundamental moral motivation? Is it extrinsic to the person, or intrinsic? Is it to be found in law, in duty to oneself, in the state or in God? Or is it to be found in the purpose for which human beings exist – their ultimate happiness with God?

2. THE STRUCTURE OF UNIT ONE

The first section of this unit begins by asking the question: What does it mean to have moral knowledge? and, Where does such knowledge come from? It then goes on to elucidate the main schools of moral thinking, grouping the approaches into the 'normative' and the 'teleological'. One of these teleological approaches – that of Aristotle and Thomas Aquinas – is then examined in more detail. Finally, the section concludes by making some preliminary remarks about the relationship between morality and Christian faith.

The second section of Unit One examines what are called 'human acts'. A 'human act' is any action conducted by a human being, in freedom, with full knowledge of what is being done, in what circumstances, and with what intention. This section also examines various principles which can be helpful in deciding the rightness of particularly complex moral actions.

Section Three examines in minute detail every single step which a person takes in performing a human act. The number of distinct steps is much larger than might be imagined, involving as it does some preliminary focusing on the purpose or end of the action, an elaborate examination and assessment of the various possible means by which an action can be completed, the role of doubts and conscience, and finally the act of will to proceed with the action.

Section Four explores the path towards moral maturity. Where are the pitfalls, and where is help to be found? Does maturity always involve submission to law, or is there a deeper level at which moral life develops? Towards the end of this section, the concept of virtue is addressed for the first time. This is an important issue, one which will be delved into at greater depth later in the module.

3.   LEARNING OUTCOMES

On completion of this unit, the student ought to be able to:

a)   understand and articulate the differences between the emotivist and normative approaches to morals;

b)   understand and articulate the differences between deontological and teleological approaches to morals;

c)   know what the term 'beatitude' means, and how it is used by Aristotle and Aquinas;

d)   grasp what is meant by the term 'human act' in ethics and moral theology;

e)   know what is meant by an 'act with a double effect';

f)   know the significance of the possibility of intrinsic evil, and the questions surrounding it;

g)   have an outline understanding of the concepts of virtue and conscience;

h)   identify the various elements that go into making rational and deliberate human decisions;

i)   be able to give some account of how conscience operates, especially when dealing with the more complex issues involving conflicting points of view;

j)   recognise the advantage of an approach to morals based on personal autonomy and convictions over reliance on codes of behaviour, like the Ten Commandments, decreed and imposed from the outside;

k)   see how genuine theonomy, based on God's rule within us, can overcome this tension between moral autonomy and autonomy;

l)   understand how this moral theory harmonises with the teaching of Jesus and St Paul about grace and 'salvation through faith' rather than through the works of the Law;

m)   know the processes by which a person grows to maturity through free, critical decisions, and how individuals assimilate inherited norms.

SECTION ONE:

WHY BE MORAL?

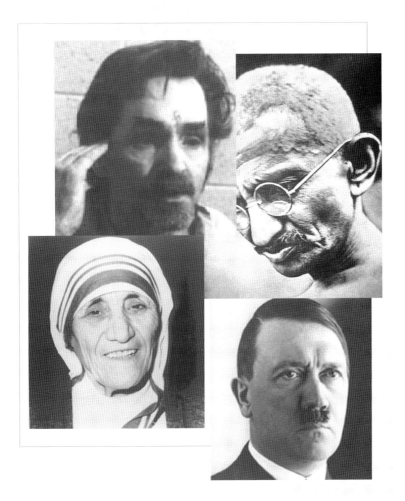

I. MORALITY AND THE WORLD AROUND US

1.1 MORALITY ON THE WORLD STAGE

The more one studies history, the more one notices that many prominent figures stand out because of the choices they made. Adolph Hitler, for example, is one of the most notable political figures of the twentieth century. He is remembered because of the choices he made which led to the construction of death camps involving the systematic extermination of millions of Jews and others whom he saw as being incompatible with his view of a perfect society; and he is remembered because of his aggression which ultimately led to the start of the Second World War.

Other non-political figures have made their mark on the last century as well. Charles Manson started a cult known as The Family which plotted the murder of movie actress Sharon Tate who at the time was eight and a half months pregnant. Jim Jones led his followers to a mass suicide in Guyana in the 1980s. John Wayne Gacy lured young boys to his home, tortured and killed them, and buried them in his basement. Others, such as the Yorkshire Ripper, stand out because of the undeniable evil they did.

Other figures are remembered as examples of deceit and injustice. Disgraced American businessman Kenneth Lay – former chief executive of the Enron Corporation – knowingly concealed crucial financial information that led to the collapse of Enron and the loss of pensions for thousands of employees. His highly-publicised trial in 2005 gave unprecedented attention to ethical failures in business. Henceforth the name Enron will be synonymous with fraud and corporate greed. In Britain, Robert Maxwell also looted the pension funds of his publishing empire leaving hundreds of employees without any hope of a pension.

But history also shows us people who are remembered not for their crimes or atrocities but for their moral goodness. Gandhi, Martin Luther King and Archbishop Desmond Tutu are remembered for their attempts to promote peace, tolerance and racial harmony, and Mother Theresa is synonymous with compassion and care for the least privileged in society.

1.2   MORALITY ALL AROUND US

In our personal lives, too, we see two kinds of people. On the one hand, there is the schoolmate who cheats in an exam or who tells his girlfriend that she is 'the only one for him' when it is obvious that he is dating someone else. Another schoolmate may spend free time working with the homeless or speaking out in defense of someone who is being unfairly maligned; and there are those who tell the truth in difficult situations, even though it will make them look bad.

What is there about telling the truth, defending the disadvantaged or seeking equal opportunity for all which makes them morally good?

On hearing these examples, one instinctively divides them into 'good' and 'bad'. On what basis was that distinction made? What is there about a Hitler or a Manson or a crooked politician which makes us classify them as morally bad? What is there about telling the truth, defending the disadvantaged or seeking equal opportunity for all which makes them morally good?

2.   WHAT IS MORAL KNOWING?

There are many different kinds of knowledge. For example, we know many facts about the world, such as the colour of an item of clothing or the phone number of a friend. Scientific knowledge also gives us a kind of knowledge. It begins with some verifiable fact and then moves on to some new knowledge by a process of deduction or inference. Artists have a different kind of knowledge; they 'know' how to create works of beauty. And craftsmen 'know' how to make a sturdy desk or chair. Their kind of knowledge is not simply factual or scientific, but technical.

Morality or ethics can be defined as a kind of knowledge, but it is different from these other kinds of knowing.

Moral knowledge is controversial because it involves a judgment about what ought to be done.

Morality or ethics can be defined as a kind of knowledge, but it is different from the other kinds of knowing listed above. Moral knowledge is distinctive because it has to do with knowing what we ought to do. This aspect of 'oughtness', which relates to human behaviour, is what makes moral knowledge different from other kinds of knowledge. It is also what makes morality so contentious. Unlike highly theoretical or technical knowledge, moral knowledge is controversial because it involves a judgment about what *ought* to be done. It is not based directly on facts, but on values or goods. In that sense, it is more similar to artistic knowledge than to scientific knowledge.

2.1   THE EMOTIVIST APPROACH

'Non-normative' moral knowledge, relies on kinds of knowing which are unverifiable.

There are a great many ways of arriving at moral knowledge. Some of these, called 'non-normative' moral knowledge, rely on kinds of knowing which are unverifiable. An emotivist approach to ethics, for example, claims that ethical statements are more like expressions of emotion. So for an emotivist, the statement 'lying is wrong' really means 'lying is disgusting or ugly'. The emotivist would have no way of verifying that this statement was true or false other than to say that it was undesirable or unpleasant. As the philosopher A.J. Ayer (1910-1989 ce) says,

> Sentences which express moral judgments do not say anything. They are expressions of feeling and do not come under the category of truth and falsehood.

(Ayer, A.J.: *Language, Truth and Logic*, 1952, New York, Dover Publications, pp.108-9)

In practice, many people adopt an emotivist approach to moral knowing by relying primarily on feeling rather than reasonable judgement to arrive at a moral choice.

Many people adopt an emotivist approach to moral knowing by relying primarily on feeling rather than reasonable judgement to arrive at a moral choice.

2.2   THE INTUITIVE APPROACH

In a similar vein, moral choices might be approached from a purely intuitive standpoint. The existence of moral judgments is admitted, but they are held to be intuitions. English philosopher G.E. Moore, for example, says,

> If I am asked what is good, my answer is that good is good, and that is the end of the matter. 'Good' is a simple notion just as 'yellow' is. You cannot explain it to anyone who does not already know it.

(Moore, G.E.: *Principia Ethica*, reprinted 1968, Cambridge, CUP, pp 6-7)

On a more popular level, many persons adopt an intuitionist approach to ethics whenever they say, 'I know this is the right thing to do, but I cannot explain why. I just know it is right.' Taboos, which proscribe certain types of behaviour without any overt reason, might be characterised as an intuitionistic approach to ethics.

2.3   EMOTIVIST OR INTUITIVE?

The outlines above do not imply that emotions and intuitions are useless in the process of making moral choices. Sometimes we 'know' something at an emotional or intuitive level even before we know it intellectually. For instance, we can have a feeling 'in the pit of our stomachs' which warns us about the moral quality of an act. Similarly, emotional joy and satisfaction can signal that a moral choice is a good one (Aquinas says that emotions make a good act better and a bad act worse). But if we rely solely on emotions or intuitions, we are neglecting other ways of human knowing which can strengthen the process of moral decision making.

If we rely solely on emotions or intuitions, we are neglecting other ways of human knowing which can strengthen the process of moral decision making.

In addition, emotivist or intuitionist approaches to ethics are highly subjective and tend to lock us into our own individual moral universes. If I say, for example, that I am making a particular choice 'because my gut tells me it's the right thing to do,' there is no way for me to dialogue with others about it. Their feeling about my choice is just as valid as my own. Hence, the basic problem with emotivism and intuitionism is that they are subjective, private and arbitrary. The only norm or standard is that of personal feeling.

Emotivist or intuitionist approaches to ethics are highly subjective and tend to lock us into our own individual moral universes.

EXERCISE 1:

Think of several examples of how emotions have functioned in your own moral life.

a)   Can you identify one case in which an emotion has made a good act better? Write 5 lines.

b)   Identify one case in which emotions made a bad act worse? Write 5 lines.

3. NORMATIVE APPROACHES TO ETHICS

A normative approach to moral decision-making is, therefore, preferable to either an emotivist or intuitivist approach. This means that there is some external norm, standard or value by which moral choices can be judged.

Normative approaches to ethics fall into two major categories, viz.,
* *deontological, which makes authority and duty the norms by which moral choices are judged;*
* *teleological, which evaluates moral choices on the basis of whether they achieve a goal or purpose.*

3.1 THE DEONTOLOGICAL APPROACH

The word 'deontology' comes from the Greek word *deontos* which means duty. A deontological approach to decision-making relies heavily on the notion of a duty imposed by the will or authority of a lawmaker. One of the most common forms of deontology is legalism, whereby laws made by those with authority actually impose an absolute duty on others to obey them.

3.2 CIVIC LEGALISM

If you are stopped by the police for exceeding the speed limit and try to argue your way out of it, they might say, 'Well, I'm sorry, sir/madam, but that's the law.' Law enforcement agents rarely entertain any discussion on the purpose or reason for the law.

3.3 RELIGIOUS LEGALISM

There is also a religious or theological legalism whereby God or the Church authorities impose an obligation on believers, and it is considered wrong to even question such a law. This is found most strongly in certain kinds of Protestantism whose adherents feel that individual human judgment has been too affected by sin to be dependable, as a result of which we must rely solely upon the word of God as a guide in making moral choices. Any other possibility risks error because of the weakness of the human will.

3.4 EXTRINSIC LEGALISM

These kinds of legalism are sometimes described as 'extrinsic' because the source of the moral obligation lies outside the person – in the will of the lawmaker. The great Protestant theologian Karl Barth (1886-1968 ce) is a good example of someone who proposes a religious deontology. One writer summarises Barth's view of deontological ethics as stemming from God's authority over us and our duty to obey:

> Barth's selection of biblical material flows directly from his basic metaphor of moral experience: the command coming from the sovereign divine Commander ... God's commands are not general moral principles founded on human nature or observation of experience. The one who receives a command does not have to inquire about its content; in fact, asking questions would be the beginning of disobedience. Because commands are direct and definite, the important moral virtues for Barth are attitudes that lead to prompt and wholehearted obedience.

(Spohn, William: *What Are They Saying About Scripture and Ethics?*, revised, 1995, New York, Paulist, p.29)

3.5 FORMALISM

Formalism is yet another kind of deontology proposed by the German Enlightenment philosopher Immanuel Kant (1724-1804 ce). Kant's approach is called 'formalism' because it has no actual content, only rules by which one makes individual decisions. He rejected the notion that ethics could come from outside the agent in the form of an authority, and proposed instead a rational deontology, or *duty-derived-from-reason*. In this view, the law or authority being invoked was something derived purely from disinterested reason, something as free from any self-serving interest as possible.

Kant's approach is called 'formalism' because it has no actual content, only rules by which one makes individual decisions.

The Categorical Imperative

*In deciding whether to tell the truth or not, Kant said that the only rule that should determine a course of action was a rule of 'universalisability': one could pursue a course of action only if one could universalise the course of action for everyone else. Thus, assuming you would not want to be lied to, you yourself could never tell a lie. The duty took the form of unfailing obedience to the authority of this formalised rule. This rule is known as 'the categorical imperative' (see the module **Themes in Modern Philosophy** for further information on this point).*

3.6 CONVENTIONALISM

One final kind of deontology is what might be called 'conventionalism'. In conventionalism the norm for choices is what the group does. In this approach, people abdicate their moral autonomy and follow prevailing cultural standards. 'Everyone else is doing it', they argue, thus failing to ask whether what everyone else is doing is right or reasonable. This approach may be classified as deontological because it places the centre of moral authority outside the individual person, rather than within.

In this approach, persons abdicate their moral autonomy and follow prevailing cultural standards.

EXERCISE 2:

a) Re-read Karl Barth's comments on obedience, above. If Catholic morality is not primarily based on obedience, what role does obedience play in our tradition? Write 5 lines.

4. TELEOLOGICAL APPROACHES TO ETHICS

Deontological approaches stress duty, obedience and authority, and tend to be based upon the maxim that 'something is good because it is right' ('right' meaning 'permitted', or 'in accord with the will of the lawmaker'). Teleological approaches, on the other hand, maintain that something is right (that is, permissible) because it is inherently good, and that this goodness is derived from the relationship of the act to a particular goal or purpose. Teleology, in fact, comes from a Greek word meaning *goal*. There are a number of different kinds of teleology, some more subjective than others.

Teleological approaches maintain that something is right (that is, permissible) because it is inherently good

4.1 ETHICAL EGOISM

Ethical egoism is the simplest kind of teleology where the goal is defined as 'my happiness' at this moment. I need to ask no more than 'What do I want right now?'

4.2 ETHICAL HEDONISM

Ethical hedonism is similar, but focuses on pleasure: 'What will bring me the most pleasure?'

4.3 UTILITARIANISM

Utilitarianism focuses more on the group, seeking the greatest good for the greatest number within the group. This principle may be applied to individuals or to a community, as the philosopher Jeremy Bentham makes clear:

> By the principle of utility is meant that principle which approves or disapproves of every action whatsoever, according to the tendency which it appears to have to augment or diminish the happiness of the party whose interest is in question … By utility is meant the property in any object, whereby it tends to produce the benefit, advantage, pleasure, good or happiness (all this in the present comes to the same thing), or to prevent the happening of mischief, pain, evil or unhappiness to the party whose interest is considered. If the party be the community in general, then the happiness of the community; if a particular individual, then the happiness of that individual.
>
> (Bentham, Jeremy: *Introduction to the Principles of Morals and Legislation* (reprinted from the 1823 edition), 1948, New York, Hafner Publication Company, p.2)

The problem with utilitarianism is that it is highly subjective, that is, it is based upon my estimation of what will bring me the greatest measure of happiness (even when that happiness comes at the expense of unhappiness for others). In addition, as Bentham himself admits, it is often difficult to say how it functions in communities, since it is difficult to know what a community is.

> The interest of the community is one of the most general expressions that can occur in the phraseology of morals: no wonder that the meaning of it is often lost. When it has a meaning, it is this. The community is a fictitious body, composed of the individual persons who are considered as constituting as it were its members. The interest of the community then is what? – the sum of the interest of the several members who compose it.
>
> (*Ibid.*, p.3)

Utilitarian judgments based on the abstract 'good of the community' often risk neglecting or destroying individuals who fall outside that goal.

4.4 CONSEQUENTIALISM

All forms of teleology are called 'consequentialist'. That is, moral choices or proposed courses of action are judged by their expected aims or consequences. This stands in stark contrast to deontological approaches, in which the standard of obedience to authority is often totally removed from any concern for consequences. Once the norm of authority is established, one is bound to obey, no matter what the consequences.

In deontological approaches the standard of obedience to authority is often totally removed from any concern for consequences.

Some forms of teleology, such as those described above, are rooted in the pursuit of what are relatively short-term or highly subjective consequences – what is good for me right now in this particular circumstance – even though the consequences I seek may change tomorrow, or next week, or in a different situation. So for this reason, the general term 'moral relativism' is often used to describe this consequentialist utilitarianism. As long as I know the goal, virtually any means are permissible to achieve it.

As long as I know the goal, virtually any means is permissible to achieve it.

While all morality is, to some extent, 'consequential' in that it has to take account of what will result from a choice, there are both long- and short-term consequences. We may choose to tell a lie for an immediate, short-term benefit (for example, misrepresenting a product in order to make a sale) and then realise later that this choice has jeopardised a long-term benefit (credibility with clients, and hence a security of employment). This suggests that there are some inherent values which should govern our choices, and that these values (in this case, truthfulness) must override the need for an immediate short-term benefit or good.[1]

There are some inherent values which should govern our choices and that these values (in this case, truthfulness) must override the need for an immediate short-term benefit or good.

5.   MORALITY AS A SEARCH FOR HAPPINESS

If morality is neither obedience to law nor reliance on emotion nor subservience to convention, then how might it better be described? Morality is first of all a search for goodness. 'Good' may indeed mean what is in accord with the law, what is socially acceptable, what achieves the greatest benefit for the greatest number of people, or what helps a thing become what it is supposed to be. Catholic morality favours this last approach, one which is rooted in a process of identifying what is fully human and in identifying what kinds of things fulfill human persons and make them better.

The 'goodness' approach is rooted in a process of identifying what is fully human, what kinds of things fulfill human persons and make them better.

This view is clearly consequentialist, in that it always asks, 'What will happen if …?' rather than merely exacting obedience. However, unlike many consequentialist approaches, it is not totally subjective because it presumes that there are some things which are truly fulfilling to human persons in the long run and other things which violate what it means to be human. In this view, *means* do not always justify the *ends*: there are some *means* which always violate the goal one is trying to achieve, regardless of how worthy the end is.

It presumes that there are some things which are truly fulfilling to human persons.

The Second Part of the *Summa Theologiae* of Thomas Aquinas is his moral theology. It falls right in the middle of the *Summa* – between the first volume on God and Creation and the third volume on Jesus Christ – making it clear that morality is not extrinsic to theology but at the very heart of it.[2] He begins the Second Part not by asking about law or obligation or sin, but by posing questions about happiness as the goal of life. He asks whether happiness consists in wealth, honour, fame or glory, power, any good of the body, or indeed any worldly good at all.

Aquinas does not begin by asking about law or obligation or sin, but by posing questions about happiness as the goal of life.

EXERCISE 3:

a) *Read Aquinas' Summa Theologiae, 1-2, q. 2, a. 8, on the question as to 'Whether Any Created Good Constitutes Man's Happiness.' What does Thomas say constitutes our happiness? Write 5 lines.*

Human fulfilment or happiness is, then, the goal which governs the moral life. This search for human fulfilment or happiness is not an arcane undertaking for specialists. It is the basic stuff of life. As soon as we begin to be aware of what it means to be human, and that there are some things which naturally bring happiness and others

1. Dr Kenneth Goodpaster, American specialist in business ethics describes 'teleopathy', or 'goal sickness' as 'the unbalanced pursuit of purpose in either individuals or organisations' and says it is characterised by 'fixation, rationalisation and detachment.' Although used to discuss business ethics, it applies to personal morality, as well. See his *Conscience and Corporate Culture* (2006, Oxford, Blackwell).
2. The Irish Dominican historian Leonard Boyle argued that Aquinas was challenging a contemporary trend that saw moral questions as merely practical applications of theology to specific pastoral problems. He deliberately placed the section on morality where he did in order to emphasise its organic connection with the rest of theology. Nonetheless, Boyle notes that records from scribal copy shops show that the Second Part of the *Summa* was checked out for copying far more frequently than the other parts. Aquinas' important innovation, alas, appears to have gone over the heads of his brethren! (see *The Setting of the Summa Theologiae of Saint Thomas*, 1982, Toronto, Pontifical Institute of Medieval Studies).

Morality is the search for human perfection.

which frustrate and hurt us, we are engaged in the process of morality. This is not just a matter of obeying laws or of following feelings, social conventions or religious belief; morality is the search for human perfection. All human beings, whether religious or not, are called to be moral, to be fully human, to 'be all they can be'.

Morality might be defined as:

… knowledge about what we ought to do or who we ought to be, rooted in what it means to be fully human.

Morality is largely a matter of seeking the goal of human fulfilment. As the Jesuit theologian, John Mahoney, points out, this goal can be seen either externally, like a road map, or internally, like an acorn:

> The objective, or roadmap view, considers every moral action as potentially a step towards, or away from, his final goal in life and in eternity. And every step counts. Morality is basically a matter of how each step fits into that movement. If it carries us forward, it is morally good and if it takes us down a side-road or even backwards, then it is disordered and morally bad … Individual acts in the abstract are to be viewed as so many stepping-stones surrounding them …

> An alternative view … approaches morality from within the subject rather than presenting it to him from the outside. It is a view of moral development of the individual which is more organic than mechanical, and more cumulative than successive in its approach … Rather than view the moral agent like an arrow in flight and on course towards the centre of the target, it considers him more in terms of an acorn growing into an oak tree. For this way of viewing the moral life proceeds by a capitalising of personal resources … by the fulfilment of one's human potentialities toward happiness … Moral acts are not steps. They are now stages of personal growth, more like rings in a tree.

> (Mahoney, John: *The Making of Moral Theology: A Study of the Roman Catholic Tradition*, 1987, New York, Oxford, pp.218-220)

This process of personal growth, whereby we become fully who God created us to be, requires at least five things: experience, the exercise of reason, freedom, vision and judgment. Each of these requirements will now be examined in turn.

5.1 EXPERIENCE

Morality is thus something of a 'trial and error' process.

Because morality is rooted in what it means to be human we have to rely on our experience to tell us what normally 'works' and what does not. Morality is thus something of a 'trial and error' process. Young children sometimes make bad choices because they do not have enough experience for them to distinguish what might contribute to their happiness and what might not. Adults who have more experience and a greater ability to reflect are ordinarily able to make better moral decisions. While we can attribute a mistake by a teenager to 'youthful indiscretion', the same choice made by a mature adult can be genuinely scandalous. 'He should have known better', we might say.

A real sign of moral maturity is when an individual profits from experiences other than one's own. It is one thing to know from one's own unfortunate choices that embezzlement is a poor way to get ahead. But it is quite another thing to be able to integrate the experience of others into one's own experience. Yet, because one's own horizons are so limited, this is critically important. This is why people often consult with others – especially with those who are older or whom we perceive to be wiser – before we make an important moral decision. If morality is not just a matter of achieving one's own private happiness or fulfilment but is rather something rooted in human fulfilment, then others' experience must have something to say.

This challenge is even greater in today's global and highly interdependent society. White European experience, which has long been considered normative, is no longer an adequate measure or the only measure of what is truly human. The experience of cultural diversity invokes the question: 'What is there in those other societies, so different from one's own, that is truly and fully human?' Such questions can be threatening unless it is remembered that to question does not invalidate one's own experience but broadens it. We are seeking the fuller truth about what human life is meant to be. This, in turn, provides the opportunity to re-examine and reformulate norms which have been based on the experience of only a small portion of the human population.

History also serves as an important source of experience. If one only relied on one's own experience of life, one's understanding of 'human' would be very limited indeed. But by reading history, one can learn much more about the human person and the development of human culture. Just as a physician can learn more about a particular patient's condition by reading case histories of patients with similar illnesses, so ever person, as a moral agent, can learn more about moral dilemmas by learning how other humans have responded to similar moral challenges in the past.

5.2   REASON

Even tiny children have experience, but they are not able to understand this until they have reached what we often refer to as the 'age of reason'. As has already been pointed out, a highly deontological approach to ethics does not always require much rational thought for its operation because its primary virtue is obedience. A strict deontologist might say, 'Don't think about it, just do what you are told!' At times, this might be necessary for children, but this is considered a very immature approach to morality in adults. A teleological ethic, on the other hand, requires the ability to understand the goal of human happiness, and to reflect on what steps might be required to achieve it. Unlike duty-based ethics, goal-based ethics always asks: 'Why?'

A teleological ethic requires the ability to understand the goal of human happiness, and to reflect on what steps might be required to achieve it.

5.3   FREEDOM

Untarnished experience is the beginning of the moral journey. Reason shapes this experience into general rules about what it is to be morally fulfilled. But the human capacity to do this can be limited if freedom is lacking. At a minimum, freedom is the absence of constraint, but there are more subtle ways in which moral freedom is limited. These will addressed more fully later on.

5.4   VISION

Morality is a process of becoming more fully human. This requires more than just experience and freedom. It also needs moral vision, the ability to 'see' the moral dimensions of reality and to envision what a fuller human life might be like.

Vision often includes more than just a rational consideration of a problem. Sometimes it requires an imaginative analysis of the situation and its various complexities. As Philip Keane, professor of moral theology at Saint Mary's Seminary and University, Baltimore, so aptly puts it, we are living in an age which has been so dominated by a one-sided approach to science, technology, and discursive rationality. Thus, at the present time we very much need to attend to the perspectives on moral matters which can be offered by imagination. The more we can do this the better and richer our approach to moral theology will be.

(Keane, Philip: *Christian Ethics and Imagination: A Theological Inquiry*, 1984, New York, Paulist Press, p.172)

When faced with a serious moral dilemma, choices must be based on the big picture as well as the individual circumstances being faced:

- a person must be able to anticipate consequences of various choices;

- a person must be able to remember past experiences which might shed light on the current situation;

- a person must be able to understand which values are at stake and imagine ways in which they might be applied in this particular case;

- a person must be able to know when a norm or law is binding, and when observance of it might frustrate the very value this norm was intended to protect.

prudence

This comprehensive moral vision is what the Greek philosopher, Aristotle (384-322 bce) described as the virtue of prudence – an acquired ability or moral skill which enables us to know what ought to be done in a specific situation. This virtue shall be described in greater depth later on.

5.5   JUDGMENT AND ACTION

conscience

When taken together as steps in moral decision-making, experience, reason, freedom and vision all culminate in a *judgment* about what is to be done in this or that particular case. This culminating judgment is often referred to as conscience about which a great deal more will be said later in this module.

A complete moral action requires not only that we arrive at a concrete choice about this situation, but having done so, that we also put that choice into action.

However, on many occasions, even after a long process of moral discernment has been gone through and a final judgment reached, people fail to act. The situation is known, the relative norms are known, the relationship to human fulfilment or happiness is known, but out of fear or lack of courage a person fails to act. A complete moral action requires not only that a concrete choice about a situation is arrived at, but having done so, that we also put that choice into action.

6.   REASON, REVELATION AND MORAL THEOLOGY

6.1   DUTY OR HAPPINESS?

Up to this point, very little has been said about the role of religion in the process of moral decision-making. This dimension to ethics has been deliberately delayed in order to demonstrate that morality and ethics are so basic to human life that they apply to everyone, and cannot be restricted to religious people.

The idea of ethics which has been proposed thus far is one which is teleological, or rooted in the pursuit of a goal. This approach to morality has been contrasted with another which stresses the authority of a lawmaker and the duty to obey. Human fulfilment, or what might be described as happiness, has been proposed as the goal which morality should pursue. Such happiness has been carefully distinguished from mere pleasure or other kinds of short-term fulfilment. Human experience, reason and vision exercised in freedom results in a judgment about what is to be done in any particular case in order to achieve the sought-after happiness.

6.2   NATURAL LAW

Reason's inquiry into what it means to be human, and the equally reasonable search for choices which might fulfill or enhance that humanity, are what is called 'natural law', and this shall be discussed at greater length later.

Natural law may be described as 'moral wisdom' or wisdom about what-I-ought-to-do derived solely from human experience and reason. This is a critically important statement, because it argues that all reasonable human beings, if they are free from constraints or impediments, have the ability to think about what it means to be human and what steps ought to be taken to become fully human. The approach to ethics which will be developed in this module is based upon the assumption that this is a fundamental human capacity and that, at least theoretically, it provides all that is needed to achieve natural human fulfilment.

All reasonable human beings, if they are free from constraints or impediments, have the ability to think about what it means to be human and what steps they ought to take to become fully human.

7.   THE RELIGIOUS DIMENSION OF FULFILMENT ETHICS

For religious believers, however, there is one additional qualification. Even though experience, reason and deliberation can lead any person of good will to know what human fulfilment is and how it might be achieved, religious believers have yet another level of fulfilment and another source of moral wisdom. This is called revelation. Revelation is God's will or plan for the world, communicated through Scripture, Church tradition and, especially, through the person of Jesus Christ.

Revelation is God's will or plan for the world, communicated through Scripture, Church tradition and, especially, through the person of Jesus Christ.

7.1   CAN ONE TRUST IN REASON?

Some religious traditions, including some Christian ones, are wary of the capacity of human reason to know anything with certainty. In their view, God's plan for us is available only through revelation and particularly through the words of Scripture. The Catholic tradition, however, holds that God's plan is planted within us at the moment of creation and that some of that plan is knowable through reason alone. Hence, all reasonable people can know something of what God intends human beings to be, even if they have no explicit knowledge of God, Scripture, or Jesus Christ. This is what St Paul, in Romans 2:15, meant when he said that 'the requirements of the law are written on their hearts.' He observed this kind of moral goodness among people who had not yet heard of or embraced the Gospel. This led him to suggest that God must have another way of communicating his will to them besides explicit revelation. This knowledge 'written on their hearts' is another way of talking about what is called 'natural law'.

The Catholic tradition, however, holds that God's plan is planted within us at the moment of creation and that some of that plan is knowable through reason alone.

The fact that Christians have another source of knowledge and inspiration about what they ought to do does not mean, however, that they live a totally different moral life than morally good persons who do not have access to revelation. Christians also pursue happiness or human fulfilment as a goal. What revelation adds to this is knowledge of another dimension of human life, one which we may describe as 'Happiness' with a capital 'H', or supernatural fulfilment. Aquinas wrote eloquently of this supernatural goal of human life in the very first lines of the section of the *Summa Theologica* which treats of the moral life:

> Since ... we are to be made to God's image (*ad imaginem* Dei), in so far as the image implies an intelligent being endowed with free-will and self-movement: now that we have treated of the exemplar, i.e., God, and of those things which came forth from the power of God in accordance with his will, it remains for us to treat of his image, i.e., humankind, inasmuch as they too are the principles of their actions, as having free-will and control of their actions. (ST, I-II, Prologue)

Sometimes referred to as heaven or paradise, or 'beatitude', this Happiness is the completion of all that God has called us to be, an end which God makes possible through the death and resurrection of Jesus.

Through our faith in Jesus Christ, and through revelation, we are privy to knowledge about the ultimate goal or purpose of human life, which is union with God. Then, by the action of grace, our human moral choices acquire a supernatural aspect which enables them to achieve an even fuller dimension of human life.

7.2 NATURE AND GRACE

There is an old theological axiom which says that 'grace perfects nature'. What this means in the realm of morality is that faith in Jesus Christ, together with the grace (or divine activity) which follows upon it, does not replace or destroy our human nature; rather, God's action in grace transforms, elevates and perfects our human choices, making them even better. Another way of saying this is that in creating us, God has planted a certain seed or a purpose in us (not unlike the 'acorn' we described earlier in this unit). By our natural powers as human beings, this purpose begins to grow in us, and by reason and deliberation we can make choices which help this acorn develop into a full human person.

God's action in grace transforms, elevates, and perfects our human choices, making them even better.

Fig. 1: *St Thomas Aquinas*

Once a person believes in Jesus Christ, he or she can avail of the additional truths found in the gospels and in Church tradition – truths which enlighten a person's deliberation and judgments by showing that there is even more to human life and to God's purpose for us than first thought. Whenever a good moral choice is made, even on a purely human level, we open ourselves up to the action of grace which then perfects and transforms this choice. Even though it is impossible to achieve this supernatural goal alone, God uses human choices as the occasion to lead people towards this wider fulfilment. St Thomas describes this dynamic:

> The gifts of grace are added to us in order to enhance the gifts of nature, not to take them away. *The native light of reason is not obliterated by the light of faith gratuitously shed on us.* Hence Christian theology enlists the help of philosophy and the sciences. Mere reasoning can never discover the truths which faith perceives; on the other hand, it cannot discover any disagreement between its own intrinsically natural truths and those divinely revealed. Were there any contradiction, one set or the other would be fallacious, and since both are from God, he would be the author of our deception, which is out of the question ... Accordingly, nature is the prelude to grace.
>
> (Aquinas: *Expositio de Trinitate*, II, 3; English trans. from *St Thomas Aquinas: Theological Texts*, Gilby, Thomas (ed.), 1982, Durham, North Carolina, Labyrinth Press, p.7)

> As daylight from the sun is diffused into the room, so the light of grace is infused into the soul by God. Although grace is beyond the nature of the soul, there is nevertheless, in every rational creature the readiness to receive grace, and from grace the vigour to act accordingly.
>
> (Aquinas: *Disputatio De Malo*, 11; English trans. from *St Thomas Aquinas: Theological Texts*, Gilby, Thomas (ed.), 1982, Durham, North Carolina, Labyrinth Press, p.139)

In the Catholic tradition believers are not called to 'check in their brains at the door' when they enter the Christian moral life. Reason and revelation are both part of God's plan for leading us to the fullness of human life, which is actually the fulness of God's own life.

7.3   THE HOLY SPIRIT AND THE MORAL LIFE

It is fitting to conclude this section with a few words about the role of the Holy Spirit in the process of moral decision making. The importance of intuition and emotion in the moral life has already been noted. The gifts of the Holy Spirit are supernatural, intuitive promptings that give clarity and confidence in decision-making. Even though, following the Council of Trent, the gifts were largely neglected in favour of the more concrete, juridical and act-oriented understandings of morality, they began to be restored to their original prominence in the middle of the twentieth century.[3] They are important, not only because they contribute to a full moral anthropology that involves intellect, will and freedom as well as intuition and emotions, but also because they help us see that the moral and spiritual lives are really one and the same.

The moral and spiritual lives are really one and the same.

The question at the beginning of this section was, 'Why be moral?' It should be clear by now that human beings pursue the moral life not merely out of fear of punishment, but as a path toward self-identity and as a realisation of vocation. Far from mere obedience to authority, the moral life is an intensely creative process. God has called us to be specific persons, unique in his sight. In the moral life, we respond to that call and with the help of grace, find both earthly and ultimate happiness.

Far from mere obedience to authority, the moral life is an intensely creative process.

3.   A good overview of the recent writing on the gifts of the Holy Spirit and their importance to morality can be found in Bouchard, Charles: 'Recovering the Gifts of the Holy Spirit in Moral Theology'. in *Theological Studies*, September (62) 2002, pp.539-558.

SECTION TWO:
HUMAN ACTS

I.   THE BUILDING BLOCKS OF THE MORAL LIFE

If living a moral life is our response to God's call to become who he has destined us to be, then our individual moral choices are the buildings blocks of that life. In this section the complex reality of human acts and the interplay between choice and freedom will be explored.

1.1   MORAL FREEDOM

An action or choice only has moral meaning to the extent that it is conscious and free.

The central importance of freedom in the moral life has already been noted. An action or choice only has moral meaning to the extent that it is conscious and free. There are many things human beings do that could be described as actions of a human being but which do not qualify as moral acts – as human acts – because they lack consciousness or will.

The term 'human act', then, is used in a very precise way in moral theology. For example, I may tap my fingers on the desk as I write, and be totally unaware of it until someone says to me: 'Stop that tapping! You're driving me bonkers!' Similarly, I breathe, I open and close my eyes and do many other things repeatedly, but unconsciously. They do not qualify as moral acts, as human acts. If I am constrained or coerced in my choice or action, then it is not truly mine. Physical restraint is the most obvious limitation on freedom. If I am bound or gagged or imprisoned, my opportunities for self-expression are obviously limited. But in the moral realm we can be constrained in less obvious ways, as well.

[handwritten marginal note: Consciousness / will / human act / act of a human]

The traditional manuals of moral theology distinguished a 'human act' (Latin: *actus humanus*) which had all the characteristics necessary to qualify as a full human act, from an 'act of a human' (Latin: *actus hominis*) an act done by a human, but lacking the consciousness or will to give it any moral meaning. Comparing a wink (conscious and free) and a blink (an unconscious reflex) illustrates this distinction.

1.2   KNOWLEDGE

Lack of knowledge is an important limitation to our freedom. To the extent that I do not know the situation fully, or the alternative options, or the benefits and risks involved in any proposed course of action, I cannot make a good moral choice. The importance of knowledge is apparent in many health-care decisions. When faced with difficult choices about treatment for an illness, we expect the physician to help us to understand what the treatment options are, what benefit each might bring, and what risks or uncertainties are associated with each. Lacking this information, we make uninformed choices. If, despite our best efforts, we are unaware that something is wrong or harmful we can hardly be held accountable for our actions.

1.3   EMOTIONS

Emotions can also limit our freedom. While emotions such as fear, anger or desire can sometimes tell us something we need to know about a proposed course of action, these same emotions can also limit our freedom by clouding our judgment. I may know, for example, that a certain business practice is unjust, but I may be so angry at a competitor and so eager for vengeance that I 'violate my better judgment' and undertake the action anyway. Or I may know that lying is wrong, but I am so afraid for my own safety that I deliberately deceive someone. Or, even though I know that adultery is immoral, I allow my sexual desire to get the better of me and compromise my values.

1.4   PSYCHOLOGICAL OR CHEMICAL FACTORS

Finally, psychological or chemical factors can inhibit freedom. Those who suffer from serious mental illnesses often have limited moral agency because their judgment is distorted by fear, anxiety or depression, or because they are actually experiencing a different reality than the rest of us. Similarly, freedom can be impaired by drugs or alcohol; in this case however, we remain morally responsible to the extent that we have willingly caused this impairment. That is why drunk drivers who cause accidents are held legally responsible even though they did not intend to cause an accident. They are held responsible for deliberately impairing their judgment by getting drunk in the first place. In traditional moral theology this is referred to as choosing the cause (Latin: *voluntarium in causa*) – they did not directly will the bad choice they made, but willed the circumstance – drunkenness – that impaired human judgment.

EXERCISE 4:

a) *Think of the best moral choice you have ever made. Were you fully free? Write 5 lines.*

b) *Think of a bad moral choice you have made. Was lack of freedom, knowledge or consciousness part of the reason you chose badly? Write 5 lines.*

1.5   TWO LEVELS OF FREEDOM

categorical-freedom

act-freedom

Human beings have moral freedom at two levels: the level of doing and the level of being. At the most basic level, we can choose to do or not to do any particular action. I may choose to drive this car, to purchase this house, to make this statement or to sell this object for a certain amount of money. Each of these choices is an exercise of 'categorical-freedom' or 'act-freedom'.

I choose not only to do a certain thing but to become a certain kind of person.

transcendental freedom

fundamental option

This is what we would call mortal sin or its equivalent in goodness.

But in addition to the freedom to do certain acts, there is another, deeper, level of freedom which has to do with who-I-ought-to-be. There are certain individual choices I make which are so serious and which engage me at such a fundamental level that in the act of choosing, I choose not only to *do* a certain thing but to *become* a certain kind of person. This kind of freedom is called transcendental freedom, because it transcends the freedom to do certain acts, and embraces the totality of my person. This distinction is at the root of the idea of the 'fundamental option' advanced by moral theologian Joseph Fuchs and others in the late 1960s.

Sometimes misunderstood as a once-and-for-all choice that renders other moral choices irrelevant,[1] the fundamental option, properly understood, is actually an exercise of 'being-freedom', whereby a person disposes their entire moral personality to evil or good. This is what we would call mortal sin or its equivalent in goodness. It is an exercise of moral freedom so profound and penetrating that it engages our entire person. A lesser engagement of freedom would be characterised as 'venial' – it is more at the periphery of our moral identity.[2]

Venial and mortal sins are different in kind. Repeated venial sins, or exercises of categorical freedom, may weaken our moral identity, but no number of them ever equals a mortal sin that can actually alter my moral identity.[3]

Take the example of a person who tells a lie. If it is an isolated incident, we would say 'he lied'. But at some point, usually after repeated lies, that person crosses the line and becomes 'a liar'. Whenever this happens, when the person's fundamental identify becomes more that of a liar than that of a truth-teller, we would say that the person has exercised transcendental freedom. He has not just told a lie, but actually changed his moral identity.

Choices made about individual acts gradually shape who we are as persons, and the deeper this personal identity becomes, the more it begins to shape future actions.

These two levels of freedom, which are really better described as concentric circles, are also reciprocal. Choices made about individual acts gradually shape who we are as persons, and the deeper this personal identity becomes, the more it begins to shape future actions. When we are young, our moral identity is volatile and easily changed: we have not made enough moral choices to have achieved a solid moral character. As we grow older, however, the choice to be a certain kind of person becomes more stable and the core is not as easily changed. Such relative stability of moral character provides the basis for character references, for example, when we seek employment. We ask those who know us to speak about who we are, because we believe that there is a certain continuity in us which enables others to predict, with more or less certainty, how we will perform or respond in certain situations.

---

1.   John Paul II's encyclical *Veritatis Splendor* addresses common misunderstandings of the idea of the fundamental option at length. See Section III, 'Fundamental Choice and Specific Kinds of Behaviour', especially nos. 65-68.

2.   See the *Catechism of the Catholic Church*.

3.   St Thomas Aquinas appears to invoke this distinction between transcendental and categorical freedom when he asks his famous question about the 'first moral act', viz., 'Whether venial sin can exist in a person with original sin alone?' (ST I-II, q. 89, a.6). He says that at whatever point in our lives at which we first have the freedom and knowledge to exercise a truly moral act, we make a specific moral choice, but only after we 'deliberate about ourselves', that is, we establish a moral identity, for the first time, in conjunction with a categorical act.

2.   HUMAN ACTS IN CONTEXT

As important as human acts are in the moral life, it is vital to remember that they must always be considered in the broader context of an individual's moral life considered together with its purpose and narrative. Jesuit theologian, John Mahoney, describes how this view of the moral life was largely lost after the Council of Trent (1545-1563 ce). He points out that the need to provide systematic training for priests who would be hearing confessions, when taken together with a number of other factors, conspired to create a new discipline of moral theology. Ripped from the theological context in which St Thomas had so carefully placed it in his *Summa*, this new model of moral theology focused on individual acts and sins, to the neglect of continuity, grace and the gifts of the Holy Spirit which had characterised the more traditional approach of Aquinas.

This new model of moral theology focused on individual acts and sins.

This fresh emphasis on Confession led to an approach to the moral life as something discontinuous – freezing the film in a jerky succession of individual stills to be analysed – and thus ignoring the wider plot. Continuity was discounted, or at most was seen only as a circumstance, and the story of the individual's moral exploration either unsuspected or disregarded. Mahoney writes:

> The pessimistic anthropology from which [the Church's strong sense of sin and guilt] started … and which served inevitably to confirm and reinforce itself, particularly when the subject was pursued in growing isolation from the rest of theology and developed as a spiritual arm of the Church's legal system, drove moral theology increasingly to concern itself almost exclusively with the darker and insubordinate side of human existence.

> As a consequence of this commitment to spiritual pathology, the discipline of moral theology was to relinquish almost all consideration of the good in man to other branches of theology, notably to what became known as spiritual theology...but inevitably this study of Christian perfection was pursued in a rarefied and elitist atmosphere more suited to those few who aspired to the counsels.

(Mahoney, John: *The Making of Moral Theology: A Study of the Roman Catholic Tradition*, 1987, New York, Oxford, pp.28-31)

Because of the merits of the traditional emphasis on virtue and the moral psychology that undergirds it, this reduction of the moral life to individual acts, adjudicated legally and in isolation, was a particularly unfortunate development. It created a distorted paradigm of morality that would predominate until the mid-twentieth century. Ironically, because of its fixation on individual acts, it eventually resulted in a trivialisation and diminishment of the idea of sin and an overall loss of the communal aspect of sin.

Because of its fixation on individual acts, the casuist approach eventually resulted in a trivialisation and diminishment of the idea of sin and an overall loss of the communal aspect of sin.

Mahoney notes that the isolation and oversystematisation of moral theology in the post-Tridentine period …

> impelled moral theology to view sin as above all a transgression of law, and has inculcated concepts of divine justice and retribution … moreover, the casting of moral theology for centuries as the handmaid of canon law has only reinforced the predominately legal approach to morality.

(*ibid.*, p.35)

2.1   USEFUL TRADITIONAL PRINCIPLES

The free human act which is the building block of the moral life is deceptively complex and as a result has prompted the development of a number of important principles which help us to analyse the moral quality of any particular human act, especially where these occur in conflicting or confusing situations. This is the 'three font theory' of moral acts which consists in:

- objective and subjective morality,

- the principle of the double effect, and

- the principle of cooperation.

These will now be examined in turn.

2.2   THE THREE FONTS OF MORALITY[4]

It has already been noted that no human act is fully moral unless it is the result of free choice. Once adequate freedom has been established to allow a truly human act, there are three fonts, or sources, of that act's moral character. These are *the act itself*, abstractly considered; the agent's *intention*; and the *circumstances* surrounding the action.

The Act Itself

The physical act itself is the object, the 'what', of the analysis. It might be a spoken word, a physical action such as the appropriation of a certain amount of money or the removal of an arm or a leg, or an act of sexual intercourse. Even though I can describe these various acts, I cannot usually tell what their moral character is without more information. For instance, if someone asks, 'Is it moral for a man to have sexual relations with a woman?' one would have to respond, 'That depends'. One would then enquire further on the details of the sexual activity by asking a number of questions.

The Intention

The intention is the 'why' of the moral act. The very same physical act, for example, amputation of a limb, would be assessed very differently depending on the agent's intention. If the limb was damaged beyond repair or diseased, the agent would act virtuously to remove it in order to save a life. If, on the other hand, the same limb were amputated as an act of torture, the moral assessment would be quite different.

Similarly, if the sexual act described above were between a husband and wife and the intention was procreation or expression of marital love, it would have a positive moral value. If the act was deceitful or unjust (adultery or rape), it would be seen as sinful.

Shooting an enemy combatant is ordinarily tolerated if the soldier acts with the intention of defending himself or others; but the same act of killing a combatant would be assessed as murder if it was carried out with the intention of vengeance or done in such a way as to cause unnecessary pain or suffering.

The Circumstances

Finally, it is the circumstances which constitute the 'who, when, where and how' of the moral analysis. The same act done in one set of circumstances may have a different moral quality than one done in other circumstances. Police are sometimes permitted to shoot in order to disarm a criminal; private citizens normally cannot; a person who disobeys a speed limit might do so with impunity if he or she is rushing to hospital with an injured child in the back seat of the car. As Mahoney notes,

---

4.   The sources of the morality of an act are described more fully by John Mahoney in his essay 'The Classical Theory of the Moral Judgment', in *Seeking the Spirit: Essays in Moral and Pastoral Theology*, 1981, London and Denville, NJ, Sheed and Ward and Dimension Books, pp.52-62.

the moral debate really centres not on the essential nucleus of the abstract act, considered as pure uncircumstanced (and neutral or indifferent) object but on the moral relevance of the various existential circumstances which enter into any particular act. They are the result of the interaction between universal principles and particular situations.

In sum, the three fonts of morality give us the tools to balance the objective aspects of the act (what the act is in itself apart from any particular situation) with the more subjective and variable aspects (intention and circumstances.) This means that any analysis of a moral act is always a ...

> process of discernment and dialogue between principles and situation. Such an approach acknowledges 'two way traffic' between formulated moral principles and particular instance, rather than a 'one way traffic' from principle to instance.
>
> (Mahoney, *Classical Theory*, p.53)

The process of moral discernment is thus neither as clear nor as scientific as we might like. It involves a prudential calculation of the relationship between act, intention and circumstances. As I deliberate about my own choices, I may find it difficult to achieve clarity and certainty; however, once having decided, my conclusion may differ from that of another person of good will. In the end, as Mahoney notes, there is an element of holy mystery even in the most carefully considered moral choice:

> There is then, at the heart of every human moral judgment an area of mystery which is acknowledged by theological ethics as the mystery of God's salvific plan of restoring and bringing all things to perfection in Christ. And this mystery we have tried to identify as the purpose of God at work in every human moral judgment ... It is this primarily, and not the 'object' of the action, 'uncircumstanced' and morally neutral, which gives goodness to all such moral judgments.
>
> (Mahoney, *ibid.*, p.57)

EXERCISE 5:

a) Consider how, in your own experience, some moral choice involved an act, intention and circumstances; pay particular attention to how the latter two aspects interacted with the first. Write 10 lines.

2.3   THE PRINCIPLE OF DOUBLE EFFECT

The important role that intention plays in giving an action its moral character has been noted, and the 'principle of double effect' is a useful tool in helping us to analyse situations in which a single action, neutral or indifferent in itself, has more than one effect: one good and intended, and one evil and unintended.

The principle states that we may undertake such an action, intending only the good effect but foreseeing a second, inseparable but unintended, bad effect. As long as my intention is focused on the first good effect, and this good effect is not achieved by means of the second, evil, effect, it is morally permissible. I foresee, but do not intend, the bad effect. This may seem confusing but in fact it enables us to analyse a number of common moral dilemmas.

As long as my intention is focused on the first good effect, and this good effect is not achieved by means of the second, evil, effect, it is morally permissible.

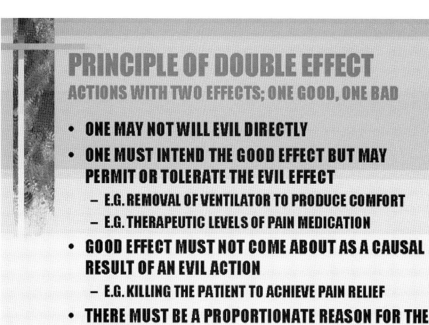

The principle of double effect is the basis of most judgments about invasive or painful medical treatments. Suppose my physician tells me that I have a malignant tumour that must be surgically removed. The surgeon intends to cut away the tissue. This action is morally neutral in itself, but it has two effects. The surgeon's major intention is to cure my cancer; a secondary effect is pain, recuperation, risk of infection and perhaps impaired functioning for the rest of my life. The physician foresees this second effect, but does not intend it. If there were any way he could achieve the cure without causing this second effect, he would; but it is inseparably connected to the first.

Another example of the principle of double effect is the just war theory. This theory is really a variation on the principle of self-defense in which I may harm or threaten to cause harm to another to preserve my own life or safety. In this case, my primary intention is only to defend myself or my country. A second effect, foreseen but inseparably connected to the first, is the death of the aggressor. As long as I focus my intention as closely as possible on defending myself, and use only as much force as necessary, I am not morally responsible for the possible death of my assailant.

2.4 PROPORTIONALITY

proportionality

One final point about the principle of double effect concerns the importance of proportionality. Even if the secondary effect is unintended and inseparably connected to the first, we must judge whether the desired outcome of the action is proportionate to the unintended evil. The value of my own life, for example, would seem to be proportionate to the risk of death to an aggressor who threatens my safety or that of my family or country. The value of my car, or other material possession probably could not be considered a proportionate reason to risk the death of another person. In a similar way, amputation of my foot could be an unintended secondary effect of treating both gangrene and athlete's foot; in the first case, the loss of a foot is proportionate to the threat posed by the gangrene; in the second case, it is clearly not. The premises for the principle of double effect can be found in Thomas Aquinas' discussion of self-defense (ST II-II, q.64, a.7), but the four conditions were finally formulated by Jean Pierre Gury in the mid-nineteenth century. They may be summarised as follows:

a)   the action itself is good or indifferent;

b)   the good effect is not produced by means of the evil effect;

c)   the evil effect is not directly intended; and

d)   a proportionate reason supports causing or tolerating the evil effect.

2.5   THE PRINCIPLE OF COOPERATION

Because human beings are essentially social and our lives are based on interactions with one another, our moral choices are rarely so private and personal that they do not affect others. In fact, in some cases my choices may not be entirely my own. I may unwittingly or deliberately become involved with the wrongdoing of another in such a way that I am complicit with it and bear some moral responsibility for it.

Formal and Material Cooperation

Let's take the simplest and most familiar case – the driver of the getaway car in a bank robbery. The law would ordinarily see such an accomplice as sharing some responsibility for the criminal act. However, if upon investigation the police discovered that the driver of the car had no knowledge of the thief's intent and thought he was entering the bank merely to make a deposit, he would bear no moral responsibility.

Cooperation has various degrees. Formal cooperation involves knowing and sharing in the intention of the wrongdoer. Material cooperation means not necessarily sharing in the intention of the wrongdoer, but still providing some assistance in carrying out the plan of the wrongdoer. In the case of the bank robber above, material cooperation might involve loaning a car to someone who commits a crime; leaving the keys of the car on the desk where the perpetrator would find them; filling the tank with petrol thus enabling the criminal to reach his destination and commit the crime. In each case, the cooperation becomes more remote from the intention of the wrongdoer; at some point of remoteness we would say that the accomplice bears no responsibility whatever for this crime.

formal cooperation

material cooperation

2.6   HEALTH-CARE ETHICS

The idea of cooperation occurs in many areas of health care ethics. Assisted suicide is a prime example because it involves the assistance of someone else to commit the immoral act of suicide. Does the physician cooperate illicitly in a suicidal intention if he or she knowingly writes a prescription for a lethal dose of medication? What if a prescription is written for pain-killers but the physician has no idea that the patient intends to take a lethal overdose?

•   Would I be morally complicit in the suicide of a friend if I chose to leave the house at the crucial moment – knowing my friend's intention but not assisting him in any material way?

•   Do citizens of a particular country cooperate in euthanasia by voting for a law that makes mercy killing legal?

In each of these cases, we see how moral agency – and moral guilt – are complicated by our real relationships with those around us. This constitutes what is sometimes referred to as the social aspect of sin.

Moral agency – and moral guilt – are complicated by our real relationships with those around us.

3.   MORAL AGENCY AND INTRINSIC EVIL

3.1   DOES INTRINSIC EVIL EXIST?

intrinsically evil acts

One of the most characteristic – and troublesome – concepts in Catholic moral theology is the idea of intrinsic evil and intrinsically evil acts. Intrinsically evil acts are those which by their very nature (Latin: *ex objecto*) are so deformed that no intention or circumstance can alter their moral character. The *Catechism of the Catholic Church* states that,

> The object of the choice can by itself vitiate an act in its entirety. There are some concrete acts, such as fornication, that it is always wrong to choose, because choosing them entails a disorder of the will, that is, a moral evil. (CCC #1755)

In Catholic teaching the category of intrinsic evil traditionally includes lying, causing scandal, cruelty, extra-marital sex, homosexual acts, abortion, contraception and a host of others. Such actions should never be directly intended (though they may in some cases be acceptable as secondary but unintended effects); they may never be used as a means to an end, no matter how grand the end or purpose one has in mind.

The language of intrinsic evil sometimes sounds deontological, as though by divine order, there are certain acts that are absolutely forbidden even if we have no idea why.

How do we know?

It is important to recall the teleological nature of Catholic morality when considering intrinsic evil. The language of intrinsic evil sometimes sounds deontological, as though by divine order, there are certain acts that are absolutely forbidden even if we have no idea why. In a teleological system, an action that is intrinsically evil is not just one that happens to be arbitrarily forbidden by legitimate authority, it is an act which is intrinsically incompatible with our goal or purpose or finality as human persons. It is an act that is essentially opposed to human flourishing. Intrinsic evil means that God created us with a purpose and a plan, and we reject that plan; God intends us to be one sort of creature and not another. If that is so, then there must be certain things which contribute to this purpose and goal, and others that are essentially at odds with it.

If intrinsic evil means more than that it is forbidden by authority, then its profound incompatibility with human flourishing must be experientially demonstrable.

This means that intrinsic evil must have some experiential quality to it. If intrinsic evil means more than what is forbidden by authority, then its profound incompatibility with human flourishing must be experientially demonstrable. If I am asked 'Why is this act so evil?' I must be able to demonstrate how this is so. This is fairly easy when we are talking about rape, cruelty, murder, gross deception and genocide. No reasonable person would ever describe these acts as compatible with what it means to be human.

In the case of some other acts, mostly in the sexual realm, this becomes more difficult. Take the example of contraception. The Church's prohibition on artificial contraception stems from its conviction about the unity of the person. It says that chastity must be based upon the integrity and wholeness of the person, including our faculties of loving, procreating, knowing, willing. We are most integrated and happy when these various dimensions of the person are unified in one purpose. When they are not, we are 'disintegrated' and we suffer the pain of conflicting needs and desires.

The Church teaches that the unitive and procreative aspects of human sexuality must never be deliberately separated.

Based on this assumption, the Church teaches that the unitive and procreative aspects of human sexuality must never be deliberately separated. To deliberately separate them, or to frustrate one in favour of the other does violence to the human person and leads to moral disintegration.

The problem with this teaching is that it is not always self-evident from an experiential standpoint. A teenager, for example, may know how to separate the unitive and procreative dimensions of human sexuality in the back seat of a car with the help of appropriate supplies from the local pharmacy.

3.2 PROPORTIONALISM

There are also some more sophisticated theological objections raised to this traditional analysis. 'Revisionist' theologians, beginning with Joseph Fuchs (professor of moral theology at the Gregorian University, Rome), developed an alternate theory which is commonly described as *proportionalism*.[5] It says that rather than viewing some acts, devoid of their intention and circumstances, as intrinsically evil, we should see these acts as possessing ontic or physical evil. That is, they have a strong tendency to moral evil; but whether they actually do in practice cannot be known until we add the components of intention and circumstances. If the intention or circumstances are good and are deemed to be proportionate to the evil tendency of the act, then the act may be morally permissible. Thus, these theologians would say that only when all three aspects of the moral choice have been brought together can we say whether the tendency towards moral evil involved in the act has been realised.

This view, which tries to account for the subjective factor in moral choices, has been firmly rejected by the Catholic Church as excessively subjective and relativisitic. Pope John Paul II, in his encyclical *Veritatis Splendor* (1993), has this to say about certain kinds of teleological approaches that are called *proportionalist*:

The teleological ethical theories (proportionalism, consequentialism), while acknowledging that moral values are indicated by reason and by revelation, maintain that it is never possible to formulate an absolute prohibition of particular kinds of behaviour which would be in conflict, in every circumstance and in every culture, with those values. The acting subject would indeed be responsible for attaining the values pursued, but in two ways: the values or goods involved in a human act would be, from one viewpoint, of the moral order (in relation to properly moral values, such as love of God and neighbour, justice, etc.) and, from another viewpoint, of the pre-moral order, which some term non-moral, physical or ontic (in relation to the advantages and disadvantages accruing both to the agent and to all other persons possibly involved, such as, for example, health or its endangerment, physical integrity, life, death, loss of material goods, etc.).

In a world where goodness is always mixed with evil, and every good effect linked to other evil effects, the morality of an act would be judged in two different ways: its moral 'goodness' would be judged on the basis of the subject's intention in reference to moral goods, and its 'rightness' on the basis of a consideration of its foreseeable effects or consequences and of their proportion. Consequently, concrete kinds of behaviour could be described as 'right' or 'wrong', without it being thereby possible to judge as morally 'good' or 'bad' the will of the person choosing them. In this way, an act which, by contradicting a universal negative norm, directly violates goods considered as 'pre-moral' could be qualified as morally acceptable if the intention of the subject is focused, in accordance with a 'responsible' assessment of the goods involved in the concrete action, on the moral value judged to be decisive in the situation. (#75)

... One must therefore reject the thesis, characteristic of teleological and proportionalist theories, which holds that it is impossible to qualify as morally evil according to its species – its 'object' – the deliberate choice of certain kinds of behaviour or specific acts, apart from a consideration of the intention for which the choice is made or the totality of the foreseeable consequences of that act for all persons concerned. (#79)

---

5. For a fuller description of the origins of *proportionalism*, see Vacek, Edward: 'Proportionalism, One View of the Debate', in *Theological Studies* 46 (1985), pp.287-314; and Sparks, Richard C.: 'The Storm Over Proportionalism', in *Church* (Spring 1989), pp. 9-14.

EXERCISE 6:

a) *Re-read the above sections from* **Veritatis Splendor**. *Explain as carefully and concisely as you can how the revisionist view of proportionalism differs from the Church's teaching. Write 5 lines.*

4. CONSCIENCE AND THE VIRTUE OF PRUDENCE

4.1   THE JUDGEMENT OF CONSCIENCE

The moral theology of the post-Tridentine period was characterised by an excessive focus on individual acts. This kind of theology was necessary for providing the detailed categories which enabled priests to hear confessions, but it tended to neglect all aspects of continuity and narrative in the moral life. It also created a certain individualistic and legalistic understanding of conscience which plagues us to this day.

Some approaches suggest that judgments of conscience are opposed to Church teaching.

We often hear people describe moral dilemmas this way: 'I must either follow the teaching of the Church or my conscience.' This implies that judgments of conscience are opposed to Church teaching. In fact, the relationship is different. While being at once both a capacity (or an ability) and a specific judgment about a proposed (or completed) moral action, conscience must use Church teaching as a source of guidance in order to arrive at a specific decision, here and now.

Conscience must use Church teaching as a source of guidance in order to arrive at a specific decision, here and now.

Conscience[6] is never exercised in general; it is only exercised in particular cases where we are struggling for an answer to a problem here and now. When the Catechism speaks of conscience as the 'inner core' of our moral personality and says that if we violate a certain judgment of conscience we condemn ourselves, it means that conscience is our last, best judgment of what we ought to do in a given situation. The *Catechism of the Catholic Church* states,

> A man must always obey the certain judgment of his conscience. If he were to deliberately act against it, he would condemn himself. (CCC #1790)

We must always give priority and the benefit of the doubt to Church teaching.

As we assess a moral situation, we must always give priority and the benefit of the doubt to Church teaching. The further we stray from it, the more risky our moral judgment becomes.

4.2   CONSCIENCE AND VIRTUE

While conscience is an essential aspect of a mature moral life, its tendency to focus on individual moral choices can be problematic. Therefore, it is appropriate to emphasise the importance of continuity and pattern in the moral life lest we fall prey to a kind of moral atomism that analyses moral actions one-by-one without regard to their relationship to a real life with a real purpose and goal.

Along with fortitude, temperance and justice, prudence is one of the cardinal virtues.

The virtue of prudence will be dealt with at length in another section of this module. However, along with fortitude, temperance and justice, prudence is one of the cardinal virtues. Like the other virtues it is a 'moral habit', but not a habit in the sense of being an unconscious activity that we may or may not be aware of. It is a deliberately acquired inclination or ability (Latin: *habitus*) that shapes future actions.[7]

6. Additional information on conscience can be found in Theology for Today: Introduction to Theology, Unit Five, Section Two, 2.6 and 2.7, 2005, Tallaght, The Priory Institute.
7. See the classic treatment of a moral habit in Pinckaers, Servais: 'Virtue is Not A Habit', in *CrossCurrents*, (Winter 1962), pp.65-88.

4.3   HABITUS

A moral *habitus* might be compared to an athletic or musical skill. Far more than the ability to play one note correctly or to kick one winning goal, a *habitus* is the enduring ability to do something naturally, readily and happily. Like other skills, moral habits are developed gradually over a long period of time. Eventually, individual acts (like all those interminable piano lessons filled with mistakes and frustration) begin to take shape as a real skill. We call a highly accomplished musician a *virtuoso* because he or she can play beautifully with no apparent effort. The skill has become 'second nature' to them, enabling them to perform almost without thinking.

A 'habitus' is the enduring ability to do something naturally, readily and happily.

4.4   PRUDENCE

Although some of the other virtues 'train' our desiring, our fearing or our willing, the virtue of prudence transcends all of them. It is really the enduring skill of knowing what ought to be done. It is the link between general principles and individual cases, between the theoretical and the practical, between the rule and its application. Unlike general speculation, prudence is practical reason (Latin: *ratio practica*).

Like the other virtues, prudence is acquired over a longer period of time through repeated choices about what is to be done. Eventually, acquired moral wisdom, or the skill of prudence, begins to shape future choices, enabling the prudent person to choose naturally, readily and happily without a lot of agonising deliberation. A prudent person is the type of person to whom we might go for advice in a particularly sticky moral situation.

Prudence is not just caution or restraint, as the word sometimes suggests. The truly prudent person repeatedly exercises appropriate courage and boldness. Sometimes the norm may fail in a particular situation; but a prudent person knows that general rules work in general, even though sometimes extraordinary circumstances demand a different solution. Nobody wants a physician who slavishly follows the medical text books that prescribe a certain dosage of medication or a certain treatment in absolutely every case. We would all prefer a prudent physician who can say with confidence, 'Generally speaking this dosage of medication is effective, but in your case, it would cause undesirable side effects.' Similarly, in moral counselling we have to keep in mind the overall goal or purpose and make sure that we adapt the norm to the reality, rather than the other way around.

As an acquired skill, prudence includes deliberation, decision and action. Deliberation includes the following steps:

*   knowing relevant facts about the present situation;

*   recalling past experience;

*   foresight: the ability to see the consequences of a course of action;

*   taking counsel from others;

*   willingness to learn (docility);

*   knowing applicable general principles, including Church teaching;

*   intuition: grasping non-rational truth, trusting emotions as one source of moral knowing; and

*   prayer and openness to the Holy Spirit.

The goal of our deliberation is not absolute certainty but 'moral certainty' – enough certainty for us to feel confident in acting. It is important to remember

The goal of our deliberation is not absolute certainty but 'moral certainty'.

that imprudence can take the form of too much deliberation, indecisiveness or moral inertia. Especially in difficult matters, we must do our best at deliberating, and then summon our courage to arrive at a decision.

4.5   ACTION

It might seem unnecessary to mention 'action', but in fact this is where we fail most frequently. We go through all the steps required for a prudent decision, but then our courage fails us and we do the lesser thing instead of what we have determined to be right. Effective prudence includes deliberating, deciding and following through.

4.6   VIRTUES IN ART

Fig. 2: *Prudence, by Michel Colombe*

The virtues are frequently portrayed in art. One particularly striking and instructive example is found at the tomb of Francis II, Duke of Brittany. The tomb is found in the Cathedral of Nantes, France, and is one of the major works by the sculptor, Michel Colombe (d. 1512 ce). Here the virtue or prudence is represented by a figure with two faces. On the back of the sculpture is the face of an old man with a long, flowing beard. He represents prudence's ability to remember past experience and to draw on it. On the front of the sculpture is the face of a young woman, representing imagination, courage and innovation. She holds in her hand a round object, probably a mirror, to suggest the importance of self-reflection.

EXERCISE 7:

a) *There are kinds of prudence that are proper to the practice of various professions, such as law, medicine and even military leadership. What would characterise family prudence, the kind necessary for good parenting? Write 5 lines.*

SECTION THREE:
STRUCTURE OF MORAL DECISION-MAKING

I. THE BASIS OF HUMAN CHOICE

The module analyses of the structure of moral decision-making. How does this fit into the more general process by which human beings come to, and carry out, decisions? How do they make practical choices that are free and intelligent? In this process how does a person discern what is morally right from wrong, and what makes these decisions morally good or evil? This will involve some consideration of the way in which conscience functions, especially when dealing with some of the more difficult and complex issues it may be required to decide upon.

1.1 BASIC ELEMENTS

Though the majority of our moral decisions may be relatively straightforward and uncomplicated, the process by which we arrive at these decisions and carry them into practice can, on examination, be seen to involve a complex of several elements. Before these will be analysed in more detail, the whole process of moral decision-making must be situated within the wider structure of human decision-making generally, along with the deliberate and free human behaviour to which it gives rise. It must first be clarified precisely where the ingredients that belong to moral decisions fit in with the elements that constitute all free human choices and activities.

1.2 HUMAN BEHAVIOUR

The only activity that can truly be classed as moral, is human activity that is intelligent and free, done under the control of free-will and directed by reason.

The only activity that can truly be classed as moral is human activity that is intelligent and free, done under the control of free-will and directed by reason.

This is the only kind of activity for which a human person can be held responsible. Such activity comes from within the persons themselves and not from any outside agent or constraints. Its moral quality will depend on whether it is directed to a morally good or a morally evil purpose. Whatever its moral quality, deliberate human activity is always designed and directed to achieve some purpose that is consciously grasped and willed by the person acting.

1.3   THE INTERACTION OF MIND AND WILL

This kind of activity, therefore, results from the interaction of mind and will in a combined operation. This interplay between thought and will is represented as a sequence of distinct acts of thinking and willing, one feeding into and supporting the other.[1] Though this way of representing the interaction needs to be refined somewhat, a series of three phases can be distinguished in this whole decision-making process.

- Firstly, there is an aspirational or intentional phase, where some goal or purpose is grasped by the mind and experienced by the will as worth striving for.

- This leads on to an enquiry phase, in which the mind is driven by this attraction to consider various ways and means by which this purpose might be achieved. If a decision is made that one of these means is most suited, effective and to be pursued, this leads to the next phase.

- The final executive phase, in which the decision arrived at is put into practice, by actually doing whatever action was decided on.

These three phases will now be examined in greater detail.

the aspirational or intentional phase

the enquiry phase

the executive phase

UNIT ONE SECTION THREE

2.   PHASE ONE: GOOD INTENTIONS

Firstly, something is grasped or experienced as a desirable goal, as something good and worthwhile to work towards. This is the starting point of every human activity or endeavour – a certain appreciation of something as desirable, of some result or satisfaction worth obtaining. This perception may come spontaneously, or it may come as a result of some earlier experience or reflection. It is more than just an act of cognition or knowledge. Our affective and cognitive faculties (will and intellect) interact and back each other up to experience some goal as attractive, or to appreciate something good as lovable, or some satisfaction as worth having and enjoying. This experience is neither purely intellectual nor purely spiritual. Often a certain emotional content of longing and desire will enhance the attractiveness of the envisaged purpose or goal.

2.1   ASSESSING WHAT IS POSSIBLE

Encouraged by this initial appreciation, the mind moves on to consider whether the satisfaction or goal envisaged is actually achievable in practice. Without some such assurance that what is envisaged can actually be achieved, no effective moves will be made towards attempting to put anything into practice. This is a judgement which the mind has to make, and in doing so it considers the challenge of what one would be setting out to achieve, the resources one has to achieve it, and the difficulties which might have to be overcome to succeed.

Hence, in making this judgment the mind needs to be backed up by a real and

1.   See. Kennedy T.: *Doers of the Word: Moral Theology for the Third Millennium*, vol. I, 1996, Liguori Publications, pp. 147-156.

continuing wanting (supplied by the will and emotions) of the envisaged goal. Only this ensures that one does not underestimate the available resources, nor exaggerate the difficulties or challenges involved. This paves the way for a realistic and effective willing of the goal envisaged and judged possible, and for a determined resolve to actually achieve it, thus firming up one's initial vague approval of it.

We do not always complete this transition from vaguely good intentions to firm and effective resolutions to actually do something. Yet this is the only thing that really sets things in motion and to keep on going until our good (or bad) intentions are fulfilled, and overcoming whatever difficulties stand in our way.

2.2   BASIC MOTIVATION

This phase is crucial in providing the motivation needed to draw us towards whatever goals we set ourselves in life. We shall see that it is here that our moral convictions, whatever these may be, together with our readiness to live up to them, actually belong, i.e. our basic orientation or fundamental option in life. This is the starting point for all our properly human behaviour. The energy and effectiveness with which we try to live up to our ideals will depend on the strength of these basic convictions and our determination to abide by them in practice. Even our perception of what we should be doing with our whole life depends on this basic disposition of our mind and will.

EXERCISE 8:

a) What is the role of good intentions in the decision-making process? How do they change things? Write 5 lines.

3.   PHASE TWO: WAYS AND MEANS

Once a person is resolved to aim at some goal which has been judged worthwhile and achieveable, that person will then go on to consider suitable ways and means of achieving this end. In short, from resolving to achieve some worthwhile purpose a person must go on to decide how this can best be done. Sometimes there may be only one obvious way to go about achieving a given purpose. In that case, this must be clearly chosen and acted on if the intended purpose is to be effectively achieved.

Often, however, there will be a larger number of possible courses to follow in order to reach the intended goal. Some of these will be more suited, and some less suited or not suited at all, to bring about the intended result. Whatever is decided on will always be a particular action (or course of actions) whose suitability for the purpose will always be affected by the particular circumstances of time and place and personalities in which it is done. That is why, except for trivial matters, a person has to reflect, weigh up and examine various possible courses of action, and to decide which of them is the best in the circumstances to bring about the intended outcome. Often there is no one possible way to deal with some practical project or problem.

3.1   SELECTING ONE WAY

A person must not spend too much time considering all possible means of achieving the projected outcome; otherwise nothing will ever be done in practice. Eventually, a person must decide in favour of one way of doing things,

The energy and effectiveness with which we try to live up to our ideals will depend on the strength of our basic convictions and our determination to abide by them in practice.

and set all the others aside. This will mean making a decisive judgement that, all things considered, one course of action is best suited to bringing about the desired result or intention.

We could never reach this judgement without the backing of our affective and emotional commitment to the aim. Allied to the mind's critical assessments, this commitment leads us to a final practical decision to pursue the course of action deemed best suited to bring us to the intended result. This is a free decision: one is not compelled to follow any particular course of action, not even the one judged best suited to realise even one's most cherished aspirations. Reluctance to follow any one particular course of action can prompt us to find good reasons for not doing so. Still, the free choice to act in a certain way is always the logical outcome of our wanting to achieve certain goals, and seeing that course of action as the best way to do this in the circumstances obtaining.

3.2   FROM 'CAN DO' TO 'SHOULD DO'

If this logical process is to issue in effective action, however, it has to move from the conclusion that this is the best way to go, to deciding that it ought to be followed. Only an affective appreciation of the present value of the goal can bring someone to make this transition from 'is' to 'ought' – from judging that a particular way of acting is needed to bring about a given result, to concluding that one must act now. Something like this has to happen in all truly human decisions to do whatever needs to be done to bring about the desired objectives.

4.   PHASE THREE: IMPLEMENTING THE DECISION

The decision to do what we know is necessary to achieve some cherished objectives does not always result in our actually doing anything in practice. A move has still to be made from resolving to do what one sees must be done, to actually doing this in fact. This is the real test of the sincerity of our resolve, and this is also where one can encounter the strongest resistance from contrary pressures and obstacles. This calls for additional energy to finally get things done. It is no longer just a matter of simply judging that something should be done, and wanting to see that it is done. We have still effectively to command or direct ourselves to actually do it. While this command takes its direction from our reasoning minds, the energy to go ahead and actually do what it directs has to come from our willing and emotional wanting to do it, driven by the satisfaction or fulfilment we expect it to give us.

While this command takes its direction from our reasoning minds, the energy to go ahead and actually do what it directs has to come from our willing and emotional wanting to do it, driven by the satisfaction or fulfilment we expect it to give us.

4.1   MIND AND WILL REJOICE

The combined input of intellect and will, thinking and willing, supported by sympathetic feelings or emotions, impels us to use our operational powers in whatever ways are needed to bring about the anticipated outcome we desire. Once a person is satisfied that this intended result has effectively been attained, both mind and will can together rejoice in this achievement and share their satisfaction with the emotions. This sense of achievement, then, brings to a close that particular process of making and implementing a decision. It may, of course, be a case of only partial fulfilment, on the way to some more complete satisfaction. In that case the decision-making process will continue until that ultimate end is finally achieved.

5.   MORALITY IN DECISION MAKING

Our analysis so far applies to all human decision-making and deliberate human behaviour. It may be easier to trace its features in some decisions than in others. Many of our actions are either so trivial or routine that we do not obviously go through all the different phases we have identified above as being part of the decision-making process. These actions originate in such long-standing and well-established habits, such that doing them involves little or no reflection. It is the same with many of the moral choices we make and act on. However, properly moral choices and deliberations must now be fitted into the general pattern of human decision-making we have just outlined.

5.1   VALUES, ASPIRATIONS AND CONVICTIONS

All decision-making starts with an aspirational phase, focusing on certain goals as desirable and possible. This first phase in the development of our human decisions and the kind of behaviour it leads to is crucial when we are considering the morality of these decisions. It is morality which has to provide the motivation that draws us, mind and will, towards moral and Christian goodness in all we decide to do. It is to this phase that our basic moral convictions, our sense of moral and Christian values and our commitment to live up to them, belong. In other words our basic inclination to live out our whole moral and Christian purpose in life belongs here. If we want to live morally good and Christian lives it is the starting point for all our moral decision-making. It gives all our moral choices their basic motivation and direction.

The energy and effectiveness with which we try to live a good moral and Christian life depends on the strength of our convictions regarding basic moral and Christian values. Even the correctness of our moral perceptions depends on the soundness of this basic inclination and sense of values. We might also see it as the primary focus of God's grace within us, received in baptism and the other Christian sacraments, and of the gifts and inspiration of the Holy Spirit.

5.2   WHAT MUST I DO?

The whole purpose of good moral decision-making has to do with moving on from a good basic moral disposition to actually achieving the purpose of a good moral and Christian life.

The whole purpose of good moral decision-making has to do with moving from a good basic moral disposition to actually achieving the purpose of a good moral and Christian life by way of the practical choices we make and carry out from day to day. At the heart of this decision-making process, the following requirements have already been examined:

a)   the need to consider a variety of possible courses of action;

b)   the need to decide which is the best or most suited to achieve the good moral purpose we have in mind; and

c)   the need to direct ourselves to follow that course of action to ensure moral goodness in whatever we choose to do.

The ability and inclination to perform these operations well and consistently will be a sign that the art of moral self-government has been mastered, that the moral and Christian virtue we call prudence has been developed. A truly prudent person will carefully consider all the options for acting morally in a given situation, will correctly select the one he or she deems best in that situation, and then decisively set about doing this in practice. This calls for clarity and practicality in the mind, but also for a firm purpose in the will or inclinations, determined to do consistently whatever is morally right, in line with the true ultimate purpose we have set ourselves to achieve in life.

EXERCISE 9:

a) Describe three concrete factors involved involved in the process of actually choosing a particular course of action. Write 5 lines.

5.3   CONSIDERING ALL THE OPTIONS

Reaching correct moral decisions often calls for reflection. A person cannot always take in at a glance the whole situation and instantly decide what must be done. The proposed action must often be examined from various angles and under different aspects. The action may also need to be related to different situations and circumstances – an action which might be right in one situation may not be right in another. One's own attitudes, feelings and emotions, which vary, also have a bearing on how one should act and react. Other events and happenings, often dependant on things and persons beyond our control, can also affect the way we should behave. This whole passing parade of people, things and events, as well as of our own attitudes and feelings, has to be taken into account if the moral decisions we make are to be truly correct and our behaviour truly responsible and morally good.

Our basic commitment to do whatever is morally right, in the midst of all these contingencies, drives us to find out what this action is and how it can best be done in all our activities. John Damascene calls this 'an enquiring desire'.[2] It is essentially a very personal affair. Each of us must consider for ourselves how we can best fulfil our own moral aspirations, as human beings and Christians relating to other human beings and to God. Sometimes we may be helped by advice from other people who may be more expert and experienced, or more objective, than ourselves. This help should include the moral teaching of the Church. But in the end, it will be for each of us to decide for himself or herself. No matter how much or how wise the advice a person may get, no one else can make the final moral decision for another human person.

5.4   AREAS OF MORAL REFLECTION

The kind of reflection that results in good moral decisions starts out from a clear vision of Christian moral values. These will generally apply to a given area of life, like business or medicine, sexual or social relationships, defending human life and human rights, or respecting other men and women in one's personal relations. The aim is not just to attain some general purpose, like living a good moral and Christian life. It is something far more particularised – like doing what is fair and just in a particular business transaction, or doing what is ethically correct in treating some individual patient or medical case, or behaving with true love and respect in one's relationship with a particular sexual partner or companion.

The aim is to discover what is practicable and right to do in each of these situations here and now. What is involved here, in other words, is not an endless reverie about idealised possibilities which might be quite unrealistic in a particular concrete situation. It has to issue in a practical choice that is realistic in that situation for the persons concerned. A serious commitment to realise the moral values should keep that person's attention focused on what is real and practicable, until a definite moral choice is eventually made and acted on. In that way the whole process of moral decision-making will be linked together – from aspiration to implementation – by a certain dynamic unity and cohesion.

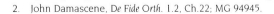

2. John Damascene, *De Fide Orth.* 1.2, Ch.22; MG 94945.

UNIT ONE SECTION THREE

5.5 ASSISTANCE IN MORAL REFLECTION

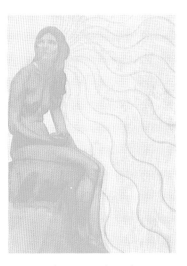

Fig. 3: *The virtue of prudence in art*

In his *Summa Theologiae* (ST, 2a2ae, q.48-49) when dealing with what he calls the 'integral parts of the virtue of prudence', Thomas Aquinas lists a number of factors that help to perfect the process of moral discernment and decision-making. These include a well stocked memory of similar decisions and situations from the past, together with a certain shrewdness in weighing up the special features that need to be taken into account in this present situation. Each person's own good sense is important for this; but it also helps to be willing and capable of taking advice and learning from other people (including the Church) who have more experience and expertise than ourselves in dealing with certain situations.

Working things out and deciding for oneself must be dictated by good sense and reason, rather than by emotional feelings or whim.

However, there is no real substitute for having to work things out and decide for oneself what must be done in each situation. And such decisions must be dictated by good sense and reason, rather than by emotional feelings or whim. There are no fixed or prefabricated techniques one can rely on for this. Moral decision-making is not a mechanical calculus that blindly implements rules of thumb. It has to be constantly adjusting to new situations and circumstances, calling for moral responses that are always unique and new. The clinching argument in moral discourse can never be: this is how it has always been done. Consequently we must never let ourselves be rushed into making moral decisions without stopping to reflect and take advice, and even to consider that our own fixed ideas about how to behave might need to be revised or even reversed.

6.   THE MOMENT OF TRUTH

6.L   WHAT MUST I DO?

The whole process of moral discernment and reflection is designed to issue in a definitive judgement, followed by a decision to act in a particular way. So, one has to decide on, for example, the way of acting best suited to realise one's commitment to justice or love in a relationship with a spouse or partner. One has reviewed various possible ways of acting that would satisfy (or fail to satisfy) this requirement. To the extent that they promise to deliver the desired result these will have won general approval. Now, however, since one can only do one thing at a time, one must choose a course of action to actually follow. Urged on by a commitment to do the right thing, one makes a final practical judgement as to what this is, and a corresponding final choice to actually do it here and now. This judgement is the conclusion of a reasoning process in which what is to be done is referred:

- first to some moral value (like fair-dealing or love); and
- secondly to the actual situation in which this must be done.

When one way of acting emerges clearly as the only one that satisfies this commitment, or satisfies it more comprehensively than anything else on offer, one's actual commitment to the value involved will drive one to conclude: 'This is what I must do (or avoid doing) here and now'. This is the final practical judgement, entailing a final decision to actually do what has been decided as expeditiously as is practically possible.

One makes a final practical judgement as to what this is, and a corresponding final choice to actually do it here and now.

6.2   BASIC INCLINATIONS

Here there is clearly a very close interaction between peoples' moral aspirations, their basic inclinations and the practical judgements they arrive at regarding what they have to do. People will automatically carry out what they judge to be right and proper, provided this moral judgement is in line with a corresponding good inclination tending in the same direction. This is the nature of practical reasoning as distinct from purely theoretical reasoning.

What our practical reason reckons to be the right course of action follows from the values we are actually committed to realising in practice, rather than from any purely theoretical assessment of moral principles. So the energy of our underlying commitment carries us through to ensure that we actually choose and carry out the action best fitted to fulfil this commitment. This also means that our actual carrying out of an action continues to share in the freedom to which we have committed ourselves and the values we are striving to uphold.

A change of attitude, which we are always free to make in relation to these values, can change the eventual outcome. We can also be assured that our practical moral judgements and decisions will be right and proper only when our actual moral aspirations and commitments, as distinct from those we are ideally supposed to have, are morally good and Christian in fact.

6.3   THE GUARANTEE OF RECTITUDE

In theory, provided a person has a basically good will, is firmly committed to sound moral values, and makes the best practical judgement in each given situation, one can be sure that such a person's judgement will invariably be right and that he or she is bound to follow it in practice. This is not to imply that 'good will' is all that one needs to be sure of always doing the right thing. Well-meaning, but misguided, people can do terrible damage to themselves and others. That is why we have to do all we can to ensure that our values are genuinely sound and calculated to bring about real human flourishing for ourselves and others. In other words 'we must do all in our power to have a (properly) informed conscience'.[3]

7.   RESOLVING MORAL DOUBTS

Apart from this theoretical point – which illustrates the difference between correct practical judgements and correct theoretical judgements – a question can still be asked about how sure we can be about the moral rightness of what we are proposing to do. Often, one particular course of action will clearly

---

3.   See *Theology for Today: Introduction to Theology*, 2005, Tallaght, The Priory Institute, Unit Five, Section Two 2.6.

moral certainty

emerge as the only thing to do to satisfy the demands of virtue. In that case one can be quite certain that this is what one has to do. Sometimes, however, the situation can be so complex, involving so many variable factors, that the best one can expect is a high degree of probability that this or that is the right way to go. This is known as 'moral certainty' because it is enough to justify a person's acting on it in his or her practical moral judgements. It means that, when one does act accordingly, whatever it is that one does is surely the morally good and virtuous thing to do.

7.1   FOLLOWING THE SAFER COURSE

Sometimes, a person cannot have a full degree of moral certainty. As a general rule, a person should never proceed to act wherever there is a serious moral doubt. Still that same person may find themselves in a position where he or she has to decide to do something in spite of such doubts. There are certain situations in which doing nothing could be even more wrong. In that situation moral wisdom dictates that a person should do whatever he or she deems most likely to be right or best suited to the situation.

This might sound a bit like what was once called 'Tutiorism' or 'Probabiliorism', i.e. always having to follow the safest or most probably correct moral opinion about some disputed question. Here, however, it is not a case of weighing up the merits of a range of theoretical opinions. What is involved here is the person's own practical judgement about what course of action appears to them most likely to satisfy that person's own sound moral inclinations. A person whose settled inclinations are basically good and Christian will naturally feel obliged to choose the way of acting they reckon will best accord with those inclinations. This allows them to resolve whatever theoretical doubts they might still have about the moral correctness of what they have a mind to do, so that they can safely go ahead and actually do it, as the right thing for them to do in that situation. For that person, to do otherwise would be morally wrong. It would involve them failing in their duty to themselves and their values.

7.2   'FINAL PRACTICAL JUDGEMENT' AND 'CONSCIENCE'

It is sometimes claimed that an important distinction has to be made between the final practical judgement that is put into action by the person, and the judgement of conscience about the moral rightness of what that person is proposing to do. It is possible for conscience to be ignored (or even acted against) in what that person actually chooses to do; whereas his or her final practical judgement is always acted on or carried out. Hence some distinction between these two judgements clearly needs to be recognised. Without this, there would be no way of expressing culpable wrongdoing or sin. If the judgement of conscience is the same as the final practical judgement on which a person invariably acts, this would appear to imply that the person acting would invariably be acting according to his or her conscience. As a result, that person could not, it seems, ever be held guilty of sin or moral fault in doing whatever they had chosen to do, since sin or moral guilt can be imputed only to those who deliberately go against the judgement of their conscience in choosing to act as they do.

At the same time, this judgement of conscience, provided it is correct, should also be in line with sound moral and Christian values which a morally good person would clearly recognise and be committed to. The fact that he or she can and does make practical judgements and choices leading to actions that ignore and go against these moral values indicates that the person so acting is not, in fact, so committed to them as to make them decisive. If they were, then the final practical judgements directing their actual activities would surely correspond to these same values and to the correct judgements of conscience. In that way, a correct judgement of conscience would coincide with the final practical judgement on which the person would invariably act. Whenever they do not coincide in this way – so that the person acts on a practical judgement at variance with a correct judgement of conscience – this is due to that person's own free choice, opting for other alternative values as decisive for how he or she chooses to act. That is why, when such a person makes a practical judgement and choice which causes him or her to do something morally wrong, that person is responsible for and guilty of the wrong he or she does. The false values that gave rise to that judgement and decision were freely adopted by the person concerned.

7.3   CONFLICTING VALUES

It should be clear from what has just been written that the judgement of conscience has often to compete with other attractions, like pleasure, or short-term gain or self-interest. These often resist what our conscience dictates as the morally right thing for us to do. Such resistance has been variously described as a struggle between 'flesh and spirit', between the 'old and the new man', between 'nature and grace' and even between 'authentic and inauthentic existence'. Ultimately, it is a contest between competing value-systems, recognised with our minds, and drawing our wills and emotions to them. The practical judgement that will ultimately prevail is that which agrees most closely with the basic inclination that is actually dominant for us at that moment. If the choice is morally wrong, we cannot claim to have made an innocent mistake, misled by a wrong inclination. The practical judgement that dictated the wrong choice is in line with the wrong inclination or fundamental option we ourselves have freely adopted and allowed to dominate our practical decisions. This is why Thomas Aquinas maintains that the virtue of prudence cannot be expected to consistently deliver sound moral judgements unless it is backed up by all the other moral virtues, which regulate the inclinations of our will and emotional drives.[4]

The judgement of conscience has often to compete with other attractions, like pleasure, or short-term gain or self-interest.

Aquinas maintains that the virtue of Prudence cannot be expected to consistently deliver sound moral judgements unless it is backed up by all the other moral virtues, which regulate the inclinations of our will and emotional drives.

7.4   COMPETING MORAL VALUES

In principle there should be no real conflict between moral values and Christian values since they all serve the one unified good of human fulfilment or flourishing. Still, the human formulations in which these values are expressed can occasionally appear to compete with one another. This is due to the inevitable limitations of human language and the inadequacy of any but the most general formulations to cover all possible eventualities. So we can say: 'Justice must always be done without exceptions' (Latin: *Fiat Iustitia, ruat caelum*); but when we go on to say: 'You must not steal nor take what belongs to others without their consent', we can immediately begin to think of possible exceptions, like a man needing food to keep his destitute family from starving to death. In cases like this a person is bound in conscience to do whatever they judge is required to secure the most basic human value, like preserving human life. This could mean having to obey a more general norm or standard, formulated to protect this more basic moral value, even if this can be done only by departing from a more particularised moral norm formulated to promote a less basic moral value, like the basic human right to own and retain private property.

Even then, the overall good, in which both these human values are ultimately reconciled, will be preserved and promoted. What a person must do in cases of

---

4.   *Summa Theologiae* 1a2ae, q.58 a.5 and 2a2ae, q.47 a.13.

What a person must do in cases of apparent conflict cannot be decided on the basis of the more immediate moral standard that would apply in most cases, but only in the light of some higher principle relating to a greater, wider or more basic human good.

apparent conflict cannot be decided on the basis of the more immediate moral standard that would apply in most cases, but only in the light of some higher principle relating to a greater, wider or more basic human good. Therefore, general prescriptions about keeping one's promises or not revealing other people's secrets or standing by one's family and friends (which apply in most cases) may have to be set aside occasionally in cases where keeping to them too strictly would endanger the lives and integrity of other people, or threaten the peace and security of the whole community. These exceptional cases of conscience call for a special shrewdness of mind, combined with a firm commitment to genuine moral and Christian goodness, in order to ensure that the right decision is made in every case.

8.   CONCLUSIONS

This combination of a basic good will, backed up by well-disciplined and sympathetic feelings and inclinations, allied to some careful and well-informed rational thinking, provides the basic structure for all sound moral decision-making. This results in the kind of practical judgements and choices that bring us to act and behave consistently in ways that prove the strength and sincerity of our actual commitment to cherish and abide by true moral and Christian values. While conscience delivers its judgements on the moral rightness or wrongness of whatever we may choose to do, its effectiveness in getting us to actually do what it judges to be right and good and to avoid doing whatever it judges to be morally wrong and evil ultimately depends for the most part on the strength of our actual commitment to the Christian values and moral standards on which its judgements should be based.

EXERCISE 10:

a) *What is the relationship between choice, truth and conflicting values in human decision-making? Write 5 lines.*

SECTION FOUR:
AUTONOMY AND THEONOMY

I.   THE PATH TO MORAL MATURITY

In this section, the idea of morality as obedience to moral norms – to rules and regulations coming from outside – will be compared with the notion that true morality should come from our own inner convictions and drives, i.e. that it should be autonomous and guided by each one's own enlightened conscience and freedom of choice. The ultimate source of this autonomy is God's rule or kingdom within each one of us, ruling and guiding us from within, i.e. *theonomy*. This is 'rule by God', not through the imposition of external rules which we are duty-bound to obey (*deontology*), but through impulses and insights God has planted within us by making us what we are with our destined fulfilment by nature and grace.

This will lead on to a first look at the concept of Christian virtue by which, according to Thomistic teaching, our basic natural inclinations, enhanced by grace, are harnessed and directed to good moral and Christian living. A fuller treatment of the virtues will be found in Unit Three.

2.   AUTONOMY IN MORALS

2.1   AUTONOMY AND THEONOMY

The real driving force of our moral lives is meant to come, not from any external code of conduct, but from within ourselves. This is what is meant by moral autonomy or self-rule. It is not an obligation simply imposed on us from outside. It is an obligation to our own selves and to our proper development as human beings. Precisely by making us what we are, our Creator gives us this sense of obligation, i.e. the obligation we experience within ourselves to become as fully and perfectly human as we can.

This is also what our Maker intends us to become as his creatures. That is why the primary expression of what God wants from us (i.e. his *theonomy* or divine rule) is not an external code of behaviour, but a kind of summons or invitation that comes to us from Him from within ourselves. We are invited to be and to behave as conscious and free human beings, striving to become what we are meant to be as fully and perfectly as possible. The moral character of our whole life is then determined by our response to this call from God which comes from within ourselves. In specifically Christian terms, this urge to be morally good flows from what we call 'the life of grace' within each one of us.

The moral character of our whole life is then determined by our response to this call from God which comes from within ourselves.

2.2 GRACE: NEW LIFE, NEW MORALS

This life of grace is, first of all, a free gift of God which we make our own through faith in his Son, Jesus Christ. It is a certain sharing by us in God's own inner life. It comes about through our personal relationship with the Blessed Trinity – with the Father, through the Son, in the Holy Spirit. It is the life that Jesus, God's incarnate Son, somehow continues to live in and through each and every one of us now. We are joined to him by faith, as members of his one living body. So Jesus goes on living in us and we in him. Each of us can say with St Paul: 'It is no longer I who live, but Christ who lives in me' (Gal 2:20).

This is the real source of our moral lives as Christians. The Christian life we are expected to live should flow from this gift of God that is within each of us through faith in Christ. Hence our Christian morality is, first and foremost, a divine morality: it comes from God's gift within us, and leads us back to God. It is also an inward morality: it is prompted and supported by the Spirit of God, the Spirit of Jesus, living and acting in each one of us. That is why it is described in the Gospel as a 'new life' resulting from a 'new birth of water and the Holy Spirit' (Jn 3:5). This 'new life' into which we have to be born again depends on God having loved us first, and having made us able and willing to love and serve Him in return. Hence it depends on faith and hope, and works through love.

2.3 LIFE BEFORE MORALS

It is only at one step removed from this that our Christian morality becomes a matter of observing rules and of performing prescribed external practices. These observances and practices should be the fruits of the new life welling up within us from God. Our new life should create and support these observances rather than themselves creating or sustaining the new life within us. Thus, for example, fruits and nuts come from the life of the fruit- or nut-tree, from the sap of life rising within it. They do not make the tree to live; and neither do they keep the tree alive. They simply show that the tree is alive and well.

In the same way, good works and observance of the commandments should result from the life of Jesus welling up from within. Works and observance are not things we do to generate that life in us, nor to keep it going. That is something only Jesus can do in us through faith and the Holy Spirit. For our part we have to let the life he gives us express itself in good works. We can neglect to do this. If we do, then we show a lack of faith, and it is this that cuts us off from the source of this new life and stifles its vitality in us.

God's gift of new life comes first, and good morals follow.

God's gift of new life comes first, and good morals follow. A fully alive Christian will keep the commandments, and neither steal, nor murder, nor commit adultery. The Christian wants to worship God and care for other people, especially parents and relatives. If, however, one tries to reverse this order, to make Christianity consist only in doing or not doing certain prescribed things, the the full vitality of Christian living will be lacking. One will even be in danger of dying spiritually, according to St Paul in his writing to the Romans:

> What then shall I say? That the Law is sin? By no means! Yet, if it had not been for the law, I should not have known sin. I should not have known what it is to covet if the law had not said 'You shall not covet'. But sin, finding opportunity in the commandment, wrought me in all kinds of covetousness. Apart from the law sin is dead. I was once alive apart from the law, but when the commandment came, sin revived and I died. The very commandment which promised life proved to be death to me. For sin, finding opportunity in the commandment, deceived me and by it killed me. (Rom 7:7-11)

EXERCISE 11:

a) *What is the difference between 'doing my own thing' and 'following my conscience?'*
Write 5 lines.

2.4 FATAL ATTRACTION/FORBIDDEN FRUIT

St Paul warned us that, instead of promoting good moral living as they are meant to do, externally imposed laws and precepts can lead to spiritual death. The law can become such a burden that it may squeeze the life out of a person, like a parasitic creeper drawing all the life out of the tree of which it is not the living fruit.

Both the attraction of sin and human perversity can use external prohibitions to prompt us to do exactly what it forbids. This is a perverse phenomenon, and when added to the attractiveness of the forbidden fruit of our own experience can cause moral chaos in our lives. When people experience morality only in terms of laws and prohibitions imposed from the outside, they sense it as something alien to their own psychological dynamism, to their own personal thoughts and feelings. It comes from other people, like parents, priests, etc., who lay down the rules. Even rules from within often derive from the inner reflections of these people and their rules without ever really becoming an original creative part of the individual person (for example, Freud's 'super ego'). Hence, individuals may come to feel that, to really grow up, they have to reject these outside intrusions. This feeling makes what is forbidden by external law seem desirable. The forbidden action takes on an added attraction by gaining the power of the prohibition, i.e. by suggesting that it will help the person concerned to become more himself, more grown-up.

How many people start to smoke or drink for that very reason? Many of the strange things immature people do can be explained in this way. Maybe they were not helped to see the values at stake in certain prohibitions: they were simply told not to do them because they were wrong. Now their impulse towards maturity, towards being their own independent grown-up selves, drives them to reject this imposition on their freedom.

The only things that prevents people from rejecting external laws is either fear of the consequences, or a positive personal application of the values involved.

The only things that prevent people from rejecting external laws are either fear of the consequences, or a positive personal application of the values involved. This is more than just theoretical knowledge resulting from moral instruction. It is an evaluative kind of knowledge, involving a real personal appreciation of the beauty, goodness and importance of the values involved. This is much harder to impart to young people than the theoretical moral instruction about obligations, duties and prohibitions. It demands a real sharing of experience designed to bring them to the same appreciation of the values their instructors ought to have from their own experience. Value is more caught than taught. So lived example is the best tutor.

The result of things being simply commanded or forbidden can eventually drive people, especially young people, to revolt. This revolt or refusal to conform is often a searching for life and maturity.

2.5   IS REVOLT AN ANSWER?

This blind reaction is, however, not the best way to find maturity. In the first place, as even St Paul admits, 'The law itself is holy and the commandment is holy and just and good' (Rom 7:12). The rejected rules are normally the fruit of long experience and reflection in the community about what is truly good or ultimately harmful. Hence they cannot be rejected and flaunted without doing real damage to the rebel's physical and spiritual well-being. Unless the person who revolts against them is lucky enough to discover their value for him/herself by experience before he/she has done too much damage to themselves and others, the consequences can be very serious.

One has only to think of the consequences for young people of ignoring warnings about drug-abuse or sexual licence. Besides, commands and prohibitions once learned from others in childhood may retain a certain secret hold over people even after they reject them in practice. This can surface later on in the form of morbid guilt-feelings and anxiety.

However, to accept such commands and prohibitions without ever questioning them, and then making them part of a person's own inner attitudes can also have unfortunate consequences. People sometimes accept demanding standards of conduct in this way and then find they cannot live up to them in practice. The conflict between their stated ideals and opposing attitudes can cause them to fail again and again. So they become discouraged and give up. The resulting collapse can leave such persons feeling bitter and cynical, resentful and uneasy in themselves.

2.6   IS CONFORMITY AN ANSWER?

By dint of a long hard struggle with themselves and their own opposing inclinations, some people succeed in keeping the rules, without any real personal conviction or insight into their rightness nor developing corresponding inner attitudes or inclinations. Such people often grimly do their duty, without any real sense of joy or freedom of ease. They often become hard-bitten and harsh with other people, as if their continuing effort to be good had frozen their hearts and hardened their outer shells.

Others may conform to the accepted conventions simply out of timidity or fear of the consequences of stepping out of line. Such people often appear excessively tame and somewhat underdeveloped. They are often so afraid of their own instinctive drives and emotions that they repress them. As a result they remain anxious and uneasy, frequently obsessed with sexuality, demanding more and more detailed guidance – just to be on the safe side. These kind of people can give religion and morality a bad name, by giving the impression that morality is only for children and spineless people, not for real, grown-up people who can stand on their own feet.

EXERCISE 12:

a) Describe an instance (personal or otherwise) of mindless conformity which had negative results. Write 5 lines.

3. TOWARDS MORAL MATURITY

3.1 GROWING IN LOVE

None of these people, neither the rebels nor the conformists, have really succeeded in reconciling genuine personal or psychological maturity with proper moral regulation. Their fears, harshness or cynicism leave them with a completely loveless attitude to religion and morals. This is the opposite of the charity that is meant to be the mainspring of Christian morality. Hence, sound psychology should teach us that genuine morality can be based only on true personal conviction and freedom, on personal love that comes from deep within the moral agent himself or herself.

Genuine morality can be based only on true personal conviction and freedom, on personal love that comes from deep within the moral agent himself or herself.

This is also the clear teaching of Jesus and St Paul. They searched behind the outward observance or violation of external commandments to the inner attitudes that cause us to keep or to break them. Indeed, real love would make us want to do all these require and more. True personal conviction about the value of what they are defending – like human life and integrity in our relationships with one another – would make us want to do what they prescribe, or avoid doing what they forbid, even without having to be told.

We are, of course, helped to appreciate these values by our sharing in the experience of the human and Christian communities to which we belong. The results of this shared experience and reflection will often be expressed in common moral standards, conventions and even laws. Still our sense of obligation to observe these will be something quite different from the unreasoning demands of the Freudian super-ego reacting to imposed rules and

UNIT ONE
SECTION FOUR

conventions. It will come instead from the deep inner drive of our own being towards its own proper fulfilment and our personal recognition, through lived experience and reflection with others, of what this requires.

3.2   READING THE SIGNS OF THE TIMES

Today, there is more need than ever to get back to this approach to morality based on personal conviction, freedom and love. People are less inclined now than in the past to do or to avoid certain things just because some commandment or Church-teaching says they must. The new emphasis on personal freedom and responsibility makes this kind of unquestioning obedience seem somewhat suspect or even wrong. So, merely reciting the commandments, or the moral law, or the Church's moral teaching, will not be enough to ensure good behaviour anymore. Hence the need to return to a morality based on an inner conviction and love.

In spite of the real danger of people using this new awareness as an excuse for doing their own thing or promoting moral anarchy in the name of conscience, in order to be faithful to the Gospel and the teaching of Jesus Christ in our days, the Church must face up to and cope with this danger.

3.3   THE LAW OF LOVE

This approach to morals does not demand that we forget about laws altogether and simply concentrate on living according to the inner promptings of conscience and the Holy Spirit with the absolute freedom of the children of God. For one thing, this freedom is not liberty to do whatever one likes. It is a freedom to love, and love makes its own demands. This law of love is the all-important requirement of proper Christian living. It is not a law that is arbitrarily imposed on our freedom from outside. It is the inner law of our whole life and development as free human beings. It is also the inner law of our life and development as the free children of the God 'who is Love'.

If we are to live and develop properly as human beings, we need to love and to be loved. If we are to live and develop properly as children of God, we must love like him in response to his love for us. If we refuse to love and to do what real loving demands of us, we shall surely destroy ourselves, by failing to keep the inescapable law of our life and so to achieve proper development.

We shall also be disobeying, and so offending God. He does indeed command us to love. Still, he does this, not just to impose his own will on us, but because he wants us to become ourselves as rational and free human beings. He wants us to grow up properly as his beloved children, to be born again into his own life of grace.

Hence, this one, basic commandment of love entails all the other commandments and all the genuine demands of the moral law and moral teaching. It also reminds us that, as human beings we share a common destiny even though each one of us must make his or her own individual way towards that goal in the company of others. Our common goal is that all humankind should return to God and enter into the fullest possible communion with him and with one another in him. This is something that begins now, even in this life, but it will not be achieved completely until the life to come. The extent to which it helps to achieve this purpose of perfect communion is the ultimate measure and criterion of the moral quality of all human behaviour and dealings with others.

Our common goal is that all humankind should return to God and enter into the fullest possible communion with him and with one another in him.

That is why Thomas Aquinas (ST 1a2ae and 2a2ae) gathered all his moral teaching (Latin: *Materia Moralis*) together under the rubric of the rational creature's return to God (Latin: *de motu rationalis creaturea in Deum*), having first dealt with God and his Creation in the first part of his work (*Prima Pars*) and before going on to deal with Christ as our way of reaching God (Latin: *via nobis tendendi in Deum*) in the third part of his work (*Tertia pars*). All of this is included under the umbrella of 'sacred teaching' (Latin: *sacra doctrina*) aimed at imparting a knowledge of God, not just in himself, but as the origin and goal of all rational creatures. We do all our thinking about morals inspired by this vision of God from whom all things come and to whom all are returning.

EXERCISE 13:

a) Is human maturity necessary before a person is capable of love? Write 5 lines.

4.   VIRTUES: THE ART OF GOOD LIVING

4.1   AQUINAS ON HABIT

Within this vision, Thomas chose to organise his moral teaching according to the order of the virtues, theological and moral, rather than the order of the Ten Commandments, though these are included too. He cites Augustine's description of virtue as 'the art of living in the way that is right and proper for human beings'.[5] An art is a skill we either have naturally or have to develop for doing certain things well, like singing or painting or playing a musical instrument.

Thomas Aquinas understands virtue, the art of right living, as a settled attitude of soul that makes it second nature for a person to do the right thing in whatever area of human life that person is operating. So he describes virtue as 'good habits that incline the person who has them to perform good actions freely'.[6]

This last word 'freely' (Latin: *cum electione*) shows that Thomas is using the word 'habit' in a somewhat different way from the way we speak of habits in English. For us a habit suggests something mechanical, causing us to do something automatically rather than freely and deliberately. So we say that someone has a habit when they do something repeatedly without thinking, like cracking their knuckles or stroking their beard. Far from limiting our freedom in this way, the kind of habit Thomas calls a virtue allows us to do whatever it inclines us to do with even greater freedom and ease. The virtue becomes something we really want to do with all the ease, fluency and flexibility with which great artists produce great music, or paintings or even great games of football or golf.

This is in line with the other classical definition of virtue adopted by Thomas and his contemporaries: 'a good quality in a person, coming from God, which inclines that person to live well and avoid evil'.[7] This description has the advantage of covering both the properly Christian virtues of faith, hope and charity, as well as other human virtues, like justice and temperance, that we

Thomas chose to organise his moral teaching according to the order of the virtues, theological and moral, rather than the order of the Ten Commandments

5.   Augustine, *De Civitate Dei*, IV.21; XXII.24, cited by Aquinas at *Summa Theologiae* I.II 58, a2. For Aquinas on virtue and virtues see Atkins, E.M. and Williams, Thomas (eds.), *Aquinas: Disputed Questions on the Virtues*, 2005, Cambridge, Cambridge University Press. For a translation of Aquinas on prudence, justice, fortitude and temperance in the Summa Theologiae IIa.IIae, see Regan, Richard J: *Aquinas: The Cardinal Virtues*, 2005, Indianapolis, Hackett Publishing Co.

6.   Thomas Aquinas, *Summa Theologiae* Ia.IIae, q.58, a.4, ad1. See also Ia.IIae q.100, a.9.

7.   Augustine, *De Libero Arbitrio* II.19, cited by Aquinas at ST Ia.IIae, q.55,a.4.

share with all people of good will. In principle, these latter values can be developed by any well-motivated human person, even if that person is not a Christian. They are developed and grow with practice, by acting consistently fairly and justly, or patiently, or moderately in all circumstances, over a relatively long period of time. Thus, acquiring these virtues is somewhat like developing a practical skill or art, like learning a trade such as carpentry or learning to play the cello. In this process, practice makes perfect, until eventually it becomes like second nature for the practitioner to do a certain thing properly and well.

Good moral qualities developed in this way are described as 'acquired moral virtues'. This contrasts with the distinctively Christian 'theological virtues', which are described as 'infused'. This means simply that we have to be given these – they have to be put into us by God as free gifts of his grace to us. We cannot acquire or develop them in ourselves by our own unaided efforts. Still, once we have them by the grace of God, we have to cooperate with, or use, them with personal acts of faith and hope and charity. Done consistently, such acts have the effect of allowing these God-given virtues to become more and more deeply rooted in our souls until such time that living our Christian faith, hope and charity becomes like second nature to us.

4.2   THEOLOGICAL AND CARDINAL VIRTUES

As we grow, God's gifts to us of faith, hope and charity will be influencing our other, moral, virtues from within. They will infuse them with their own distinctive Christian spirit and open them up to the gift and fruits of the Holy Spirit. This will then give these natural moral virtues a properly Christian character in tune with the virtues of faith, hope and charity which come to us in the first place as gifts of God's grace. As a result, when we are being fair in our dealings with other people, for example, we are not just prompted by human justice, but also by Christian charity.

The people whose rights we respect in justice, we treat as our brothers and sisters in Christ, loved by us with the same love with which we love God our Father and Jesus His Son and our brother. When we hold our temper with someone who is causing us great annoyance, we are also going further than just exercising ordinary human restraint. Our faith in Jesus' triumph over evil and death makes us able to imitate his superhuman patience. Again, when we show courage in the face of sickness and death, our hope in the risen Jesus makes this something more than just putting up a humanly brave front in the face of adversity. Our human courage is buoyed up by the Holy Spirit's gift of fortitude (or courage) and is inspired by the beatitude announced by Jesus, 'blessed are those who mourn, for they shall be comforted' (Mt 5:4).

In that way all the different virtues working together in our Christian lives can cause each of us to realise in our own way the claim made by St Paul that,

> it is no longer I who live, but Christ who lives in me. (Gal 2:20)

While the properly Christian theological virtues of faith, hope and charity help us more directly, though not exclusively, in our relations with God, the so-called 'moral' virtues have to do more directly (though again, not exclusively) with how we behave towards ourselves and other persons. The principal moral virtues are called the cardinal virtues of prudence, justice, fortitude (courage) and temperance. The title 'cardinal' has no connection with the cardinals of the Roman Church as if these eminent personages were specially noted for the practice of these virtues. The title is derived from the Latin word for a hinge, *cardo*, because these are the four key moral virtues around which all the other moral virtues revolve.

4.3   PRESIDING VIRTUES

Each of these virtues has a family of lesser but no less important virtues grouped around it. These tend to be specialisations of one of the four cardinal virtues. Each of them targets a particular sphere of human activity covered by the presiding cardinal virtue, like justice or temperance. So, for example, under the umbrella of the cardinal virtue of temperance (moderation), which regulates the whole area of pleasure and enjoyment, we find a little-known virtue called *eutrapelia*, which moderates our enjoyment of sports and games in such a way as to give their enjoyment its due place in our busy lives.

While each of the virtues can be studied and talked about by itself, we should remember that all our Christian and moral virtues are linked and interact with one another in various ways to bring about a certain organised unity in our lives. Thus the cardinal virtue of prudence presides over all our moral virtues, to help us discern how we can best practise these other virtues in different circumstances.

Love for God and neighbour makes us want to do what is best for them in every situation. But love alone will not tell us what that is precisely. Well-meaning people can wreak havoc and do terrible damage, unless they are guided by prudence.

4.4   GOOD INCLINATIONS

The most basic principle for our moral lives is 'do good, and avoid evil'. This is also one of our basic moral inclinations as human beings, to look for whatever is good for ourselves and for others, and to try to avoid whatever is bad and harmful to us. This does not stop us from sometimes choosing things that are evil or bad for us; otherwise there would be no sin in our lives. Sinning means deliberately choosing what we know is wrong or evil. Still, whenever we choose something bad, it is not because it is evil or bad that we choose it. We choose it for the good we see, or think we see, in it, whether for ourselves or for others.

This means we do not choose evil because it is evil or bad, but because it appears good to us at the time. So, for example, we can choose to tell lies, not because lying is wrong or bad, but because it gets us out of trouble, or brings us some other advantage. Because this appears good to us at the time, we are prepared to accept the wrong we know goes with it for the sake of the good we expect to gain from it. That is how we sin, by committing some deliberate wrongdoing. To avoid this we need to be able to discern what is really good, though it is in fact wrong or evil. Prudence gives us the discernment to see clearly the genuine good we have to do in every instance and the determination to get it done in practice.

Whenever we choose something bad, it is not because it is evil or bad that we choose it. We choose it for the good we see, or think we see, in it, whether for ourselves or for others.

4.5   VIRTUES WORKING TOGETHER

Prudence, if it is to be effective in getting us to do the right thing consistently, needs to be backed up by good inclinations in our will and affective powers. These will incline us to choose consistently what is truly good, like love, or fairness in our dealings with others, rather that what is evil which has presented itself to us as a good at the time, like lustful pleasure or dishonest gains from sharp practice. The good inclinations which the other moral virtues will give us are:

- Justice, for example, will incline our wills to give other people what is rightfully theirs, rather than cheat them of their rights for our own advantage.

- Temperance (moderation) will keep our bodily desires for pleasure and satisfaction within the proper bounds and prevent them from going to harmful excess, for example by causing us to eat or drink too much.

- Fortitude (courage) will restrain our fears and similar emotions, so that they don't impel us to sacrifice what is truly good for us in order to secure some apparent good, like false security.

These three, along with prudence, make up the four cardinal virtues: prudence, justice, fortitude and temperance.

EXERCISE 14:

a) What is the difference between the theological and the cardinal virtues? Write 5 lines.

CONCLUSIONS TO UNIT ONE

I.   FREEDOM AND INDEPENDENCE

This first unit on fundamental moral theology has covered a wide area. It began by distinguishing the main branches of moral and ethical thinking which one finds in the world today. These moral or ethical theories – emotivist or normative, deontological or teleological, etc. – can be found among moral or ethical thinkers be they philosophers or theologians, religious or secular. Indeed, some of the theories outlined in this unit have already come up in other modules of this programme such as those on *Introduction to Theology* and *Themes in Modern Philosophy*. A great deal of moral theory spans the religious and secular divide.

But what is particularly noteworthy about current trends in moral thinking is the tendency for many theologians and some philosophers to return to the ethical theories of Aristotle and Aquinas. Leading ethical theorists such as the Scottish philosopher, Alasdair MacIntyre (b. 1929 ce) have pioneered a fresh appraisal to 'virtue ethics', even though many Christian moral theologians had never abandoned it.

The unit has also analysed the concept of the 'human act', and has noted salient features of human life such as freedom and knowledge and intention as being essential aspects of human acts for which human beings are held to be responsible. The concept of the human act is foundational for Christian moral theology precisely because it emphasises such freedom and responsibility.

The third section of the unit has analysed in detail every step involved in the performance of a single human act. It ranges through concepts of intention, aim or end, choice of means, attainability, conscience, implementation, doubts,

resolving doubts, implementation, etc. It is only when analysed in this minute fashion that the complexity of moral decision-making can be fully exposed, and the steps and concepts involved come to light.

Section Four of the unit focused on the concept of autonomy, or what might be called in modern language maturity and independence. By embracing the concept of virtue, Catholic moral thinking has embraced this concept of individual, personal maturity.

2.   LEARNING OUTCOMES ASSESSED

By the end of this unit, the student should have a good knowledge of:

a)   the range of moral theories currently in use by philosophers and theologians, which of these are favoured by Catholic and Christian theologians and why;

b)   the term 'human act', what it involves, and why it is important;

c)   the decisive elements which together make up a single, human act;

d)   an outline idea of virtue, and why the virtue of prudence is of special importance;

e)   the role of conscience; and

f)   the contrast between a morality based on autonomy and conviction, and one based on a reliance on codes of behaviour imposed from the outside.

UNIT ONE
CONCLUSIONS

NATURE, REASON, LAW AND GROWTH

INTRODUCTION TO UNIT TWO

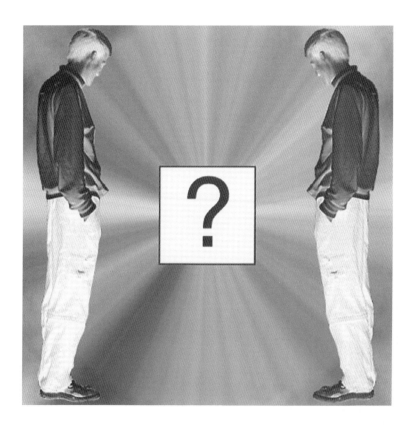

1. LAW AND NATURE, GRACE AND REASON

This second unit of the module on Fundamental Moral Theology is dominated by two words: nature and law, and the words grace and reason are not far behind. The words nature and law can have very different meanings when used in different contexts, especially if one of those contexts is theology. A believer looks at the world as the creation of God, and in doing so attributes to God the creative actions which govern the world. This creativity is a type of law, but not the same type of law which we meet in a parliment or a court-room. It is only by analogy that it is called law. In addition, what of the word nature? Who decides what is natural and what is unnatural? and what difference does the answer to this question make to a moral theology?

2. THE CONTENT OF UNIT TWO

Section One of this unit looks at the whole relationship between morality and law. Are they the same, or is morality other than law? Do all moral philosophers and theologians agree on this point? What are the essential aspects of law, and how does one's moral outlook change if one places laws and the duty to obey them at the summit of a moral theology? The section then looks at the role which reason plays in law. What is canon law, or Church law? And in what way does it differ from secular law? Who makes laws, and on what basis? Are there laws we receive from God; and if so how? Can laws be unreasonable? What is the role of Church law? These and many more questions are asked before the section relates the question of law to that of moral responsibility. The relationship between law, conscience and grace is explored towards the end of the section. How does the Bible look on law, especially the Old Testament which begins with five books collectively known as 'The Law'; Is this the same type of law that St Paul brushes aside in the Letter to the Galatians?

Section Two then explores what is meant by 'natural law'. Is natural law the same type of law as the laws which are made by politicians? Is natural law from God? The section explores the history of the concept of natural law, even where it exists under other names. Does the concept of natural law have a different role in Catholic and Protestant theology, and how does the Catholic view of natural law relate to the Scriptures when it comes to finding answers to complex moral issues?

Section Three looks at the question of moral and intellectual development in human beings. But instead of using the concepts and categories of philosophy for the task, it is the experimental results of the work of Jean Piaget and Lawrence Kohlberg which form the backbone of this study.

3.   LEARNING OUTCOMES

By the end of this unit, the student should be able to:

a)   articulate how different moral theologies have differing relationships to the concept of law;

b)   understand that canon law has a unique place in society, and has its own structure, norms and content;

c)   know what role human reason plays in the creation and following of laws;

d)   be clear on what the concept of natural law means, and why it is important for some schools of moral thinking;

e)   see the relationship which a morality based on natural law establishes for particular moral issues such as justice, sexual relations and health-care issues;

f)   relate natural law to revelation in a manner which respects both sources; and

g)   be able to follow the modern research done in the twentieth century by scholars such as Piaget and Kohlberg, and understand how their results endorse a great deal of earlier philosophical and theological thinking.

SECTION ONE
MORALITY AND LAW

Fig. 4: *The Ten Commandments*

I.   FUNDAMENTAL IDEAS ABOUT LAW

At midday prayer of the Divine Office, the Church says the following prayer over and over, month after month,

> Oh, how I love your law!
> It is my meditation all day long.
> Your commandment makes me wiser than my enemies,
> for it is with me always. (Ps. 119:97)

However, the Lectionary of the Mass also reminds us with regularity of these cautionary words of the Saviour:

> The Sabbath was made for humankind, and not humankind for the Sabbath; so the Son of Man is Lord even of the Sabbath. (Mk 2:27)

These texts combine love for God's law and docility before God's law together with critical thought and clear-minded discernment about legal institutions. Both movements pertain to a healthy Christian moral life.

These familiar passages from sacred scripture show us two contrasting glimpses of law and how the human heart responds differently to different ideas of law in different situations. In the first case, the psalmist rhapsodises with a spirit of confidence and gratitude concerning what a blessing it is for someone to have such a close relationship with God – to know God's will and have God's help in making sense out of life. By contrast, the second passage from the Gospel of Mark, in a situation where Jesus was in conflict with the Pharisees who were interpreting the law unreasonably, gave Mark the opportunity to articulate a principle of great importance for interpreting laws, even biblical laws.

Human beings were not created in order to measure their life by obeying laws; laws are given in order to help human beings find meaning in their lives.

This section on the relationship between law and morality begins with a recognition of the tension between, on the one hand, law as a benevolent and gracious manifestation of divine wisdom, and, on the other hand, law as a legalistic contraction of human freedom. There is truth to both sides of the contrasting picture.

1.1   TROUBLES WITH THE IDEA OF LAW

Today, in western capitalist cultures, law and lawyers are not highly prized (although highly paid). Law is intended to make the possibilities for cooperation amongst a multitude of people living together in a society clear and attractive, especially in societies which have inherited age-old traditions and values. This aspect of law as tradition is complicated for us by the existing and growing cultural pluralism of our cities and countries. In the face of this pluralism, there are multiplying claims for the rights of individual groups, often leading to litigation over issues of non-traditional rights. Lawyers who are willing to espouse almost any sort of litigation have not given their profession or the law a very good name.

The aspect of law as tradition is complicated by the existing and growing cultural pluralism of our cities and countries.

The reputation of legislators does not fare much better. People often get elected to represent their constituents by the support of special interest groups. Hence, legislators are less likely to have a genuine concern for bringing harmony to the diverse interests of society than they are to promote the interests of their sponsors who demand privileges for certain groups. As a consequence, the very people who should represent the dignity and power of the law as a reconciling and unifying force, often bring it into low repute and therefore stimulate a cynicism about the legal system.

Both civil society and the Church are faced with imposing structures of law – civil law and canon law. It doesn't demand too much reflection to recognise the necessity for structures which will maintain good order in the national and international organisations of State or Church. This order sometimes needs to be imposed, because a multiplicity of wills means the likelihood of varying opinions about what is needed for the good of society.

There is an unstated presumption in contemporary societies that morality is essentially about obligations, and that obligations are established by laws. In the end it will be clear that this presumption is erroneous because it is too simplistic and too extrinsic to personal moral growth.

By contrast with a general tendency today to disdain or disregard the role of law, Catholic moral theology has a healthy respect for law; but it also has a perspective on law that is quite different from the prevailing popular notions in western culture.

The tast of this section is to take the necessary steps to establish a healthy appreciation for the meaning of law that is in accord with good theology. By contrast with a general tendency today to disdain or disregard the role of law, Catholic moral theology has a healthy respect for law; but it also has a perspective on law that is quite different from the prevailing popular notions in western culture. It is worthwhile sorting this out.

1.2   AQUINAS ON LAW

Eleonore Stump, one of today's leading commentators on Aquinas' thought summarises his views on law as follows.

Stump, Eleonore: *Aquinas*, 2003, London, Routledge, pp 25-6.

In the Summa Theologiae (ST Iallae qq.90-180), Thomas Aquinas gives a famous and original treatment of the subject of law. The best-known feature of this treatise is his concept of natural law, but before embarking on that particular topic, Aquinas defines law in general as follows.

> *Law is a kind of rational ordering for the common good, promulgated by the one who takes care of the community ...*

> *The precepts of the natural law are to practical reasoning what the first principles of demonstrations are to theoretical reasoning ... all things to be done or to be avoided pertain to the precepts of natural law, which practical reasoning apprehends naturally as being human goods. (ST Iallae, 94.2)*

Human laws of all kinds derive, or should derive, from natural law, which might be construed as the naturally knowable rational principles underlying morality in general:

> *From the precepts of the natural law, as from general, indemonstrable principles, it is necessary that human reason proceed to making more particular arrangements ... [which] are called laws, provided that they pertain to the definition (ratio) of the law already stated. (Iallae, 91.3)*

As a consequence of this hierarchy of laws, Aquinas unhesitatingly rejects some kinds of and some particular instances of human law, for example:

> *A tyrannical law, since it is not in accord with reason, is not unconditionally a law but is, rather, a perversion of law. (Iallae. 92.1.ad4)*

Even natural law rests on the more fundamental concept of 'eternal law' which Aquinas identifies as divine providence, 'the very nature of the governance of things on the part of God as ruler of the universe' (Iallae. 91.1).

2.   AUTONOMY AND HETERONOMY

2.1   AUTHENTICITY AND INTIMIDATION

Another section of this module emphasises the importance of defining a human act as an internally motivated action that is clearly understood and willingly undertaken. In the language of moral philosophy, this kind of action is referred to as 'autonomous', that is, an action that is produced from within the person. From Greek roots, the word autonomy means 'law' (Greek: *nomos*), coming from the 'self' (Greek: *autos*).

Catholic moral theology is concerned not simply with favouring moral actions imbued with this quality of internal motivation, but also with developing moral agents whose whole lives are characterised by this quality of intelligence and freedom – autonomous persons. It takes an autonomous person to relate in a healthy way to the law.

By contrast with autonomy we speak of 'heteronomy' as behaviour which is governed not by an internally conceived sense of direction, but by the insistence of someone else. When a person acts out of a constrained obedience to the law – even where one ends up doing what is right – the act is heteronomous (Greek: *nomos* = law or rule; Greek: *heteros* = other). An ethos of legalism and constraint will produce moral agents whose understanding and inclinations are guided by blind obedience and taken-for-granted submission – heteronomous persons. While there are authorities and legislators at work in today's society whose goal is to establish among the people a heteronomous relation to law; that is the opposite of the position of Catholic moral theology. All good laws must be in the service of educating free persons capable of initiative and creative moral action.

While there are authorities and legislators at work in today's society whose goal is to establish among the people a heteronomous relation to law; that is the opposite of the position of Catholic moral theology.

Another unit of this module examines the genesis of autonomy in moral development. But for the present, the contrast between autonomy and heteronomy as moral qualities will be clarified. As the relation between law and morality is further examined, the goal of any good law to foster autonomy will be kept in mind; i.e., to favour the development of genuine 'human acts' in the proper sense of the term.

The characteristics of autonomous persons include:

- clear understanding;
- a willing internalisation of the community's customs and traditions;
- an eagerness to enter into productive social activity;
- a clear sense of purpose; and
- a *joie de vivre* – living life in a way that makes sense.

Autonomous persons are creative persons because they are clear about where they are going and free to find ways to achieve their objectives with imagination and self-interest. To understand the meaning of law properly, one should remember that laws are meant for autonomous persons – or at least are meant to help produce autonomous persons. Likewise, we can understand that there is something wrong about a picture in which laws produce fear, blind obedience and passivity. Put more simply, good laws foster autonomy. Laws that foster dependence and heteronomy are bad laws.

EXERCISE 1:

a) *What do you know about the meaning of autonomy and heteronomy? Write 5 lines.*

b) *Think about moments when you have been treated in a childish way by authorities? Why did you suffer a lack of respect? Can you understand heteronomy as the consequence of being put down in such manner or limited in your responses to a situation that you considered important? Write 5 lines.*

c) *At what point do you make the most positive contribution in your work or in your relationships? Do you find yourself excited and enhanced by the opportunity to make a personal contribution? Can you see how the idea of autonomy plays into this sort of freedom of expression and enthusiastic investment of the self? Write 5 lines.*

d) *Make a short list of things in the life of the Church (especially in your parish) that promote heteronomy, and of those that promote automony? If convenient, discuss these insights with someone else and listen to their reactions and response. Write 5 lines.*

3. DESCRIBING LAW

3.1 ESSENTIAL ASPECTS OF LAW

There are a number of different ways of explaining the essential meaning of law and, as we shall see, there are two rival accounts in Catholic theology about law's meaning. Here we will follow a few steps that will allow us first to understand the meaning of law in any tradition, and which will then allow us to proceed to the understanding of law that is emerging in the current renewal of moral theology (under the influence of a return to the central importance of the virtues for the moral life). The explanation that follows is largely indebted to the theological perspective of Thomas Aquinas and of contemporary exponents of his vision of morality. So what will be done next will be to skim over the surface of a highly complicated theological tradition.

3.2 HUMAN NECESSITY

It is best to begin by recognising that the way human beings have been created necessitates that they engage in a great deal of reflection and choice at significant moments of any action. That is the way the human being is made: this can be called an anthropology of law. Put another way, human beings either implicitly or explicitly arrive at norms in the process of proceeding to act. Such is the nature of human freedom that people are obliged to use their liberty, and even when they refuse to do so, their refusal is already a choice not to act in a certain way. The necessity to make a decision, far from being a burden extrinsic to freedom, is what gives meaning to freedom in the first place. It is a psychological or anthropological necessity in the sense that human beings are made to reflect on their possibilities and to elect one or other of the concrete options which they find posed before them. Choices are made by individuals based on a weighing of their desires and their commitments.

Such is the nature of human freedom: people are obliged to use their liberty, and even when they refuse to do so, their refusal is already a choice not to act in a certain way.

Sometimes this process is nearly unconscious or automatic, especially when the matter in question is at hand and is routine and not particularly important. At other times, however, something more serious must be decided and the process of reflection and decision may seem difficult, obscure and even painful. Nonetheless, arriving at a norm that directs the action of the person to actually do something pertains to the very nature of our moral endowment. For the sake of argument, by equating 'law' and 'norm of reason' in this instance, we can say that at this basic level of human morality, human beings cannot escape laws. It is in their nature to generate them and to follow them. People always want to know what they should do, and why.

Human beings cannot escape laws. It is in their nature to generate them and to follow them.

3.3 THE LAW OF REASON

As is also clear in the remarks just made, every law is in some way the result of a process of reasoning or, as medieval theology described it, an 'ordering of reason'. Reason, in this simplest sense, means whatever conforms to the logic of the situation, whatever appears sensible to the human mind.

One property of reason is to perceive the link between 'means' and 'ends'. A rational choice, therefore, is the choice of one of several possibilities, a choice made on the basis of its being the best means to achieve an end that is good for the person. Often the end to be achieved is not easy to perceive, and we must make several attempts at finding our way – falling sometimes into error and having to repeat ourselves – before we ever discover the true way. We all make mistakes, but generally speaking we learn by our mistakes. Ultimately, however, it is our over-arching or most important goals that shape our actions and structure our reasoning in our moral reflection.

One property of reason is to perceive the link between 'means' and 'ends'. A rational choice, therefore, is the choice of one of several possibilities, a choice made on the basis of its being the best means to achieve an end that is good for the person.

Fig. 5: *Goya - 'The sleep of reason produces monsters'*

The first form of moral law, therefore, is reason itself, which governs the choice of our actions in conformity with our search for a meaningful and purposeful life. This process of *discerning* in order to act for a good end is exactly what we mean by moral conscience, a subjective norm exercised in relation to our experiences and our abilities to act. The skills needed for the ordering of moral reason are:

- learning to respect and cooperate with others;

- honouring the common commitments that belong to members of a community; and

- discovering how to prioritise objectives and goals of different weight so as to choose the best.

Moral reason always seeks to situate itself in autonomy, that is, to preserve an internal principle of guidance and a spirit of freedom.

Nonetheless, we can see from this analysis that moral reason always seeks to situate itself in autonomy, that is, it seeks to preserve an internal principle of guidance and a spirit of freedom.

3.4   THE COMMON GOOD

As must be obvious, law is not concerned primarily with individual matters, but with social affairs. That is because the human person is fundamentally social. No one can exist outside of a society – with its resources of mutual help, education, protection and cultural enrichment. Further, as we will see in the following section concerning moral development, each person has a history of social and moral growth which profoundly affects their capacity to understand and evaluate individual choices. One of the principal responsibilities of society is to educate its citizens to a productive life in community. Put in technical language, society has the responsibility to promote the common good. When members of a society internalise the procedures and values that benefit the whole, we say that they have learned to act for the common good.

Society has the responsibility to promote the common good.

This idea of the common good is opposed to certain ideas of the person as being fundamentally independent and separate from society, who only enters into society by contract, and only if it is to the individual's personal advantage. In an age of globalisation, this individualistic understanding of the role of the person in society clearly underlies the spirit of capitalism. Such a concept of society dissolves responsibility for the well-being of other, weaker, members of the social order.

The concept of the common good forms the basis for both society's claims on the individual and the individual's claim on society. The principles of Catholic social teaching will be examined later in this module; but they will be seen to be rooted precisely in the social nature of the human person and in the relationship that exists between rich and poor, the gifted and less gifted, which results from our human solidarity as creatures of the one same loving God.

In order to achieve a just and fair distribution of wealth, society has the right to create institutions and to impose laws upon its members. Such laws are referred to as positive laws, meaning that it is the result of a process of legislation and juridical surveillance. Vatican II's *Pastoral Constitution on the Church in the Modern World* expresses this reality as follows:

positive law

The concrete forms of structure and organisation of public authority adopted in political communities will vary according to people's differing characters and historical developments; but their aim should always be the formation of human persons who are cultured, peace-loving, and well disposed toward all, to the benefit of the whole human race.

(The Church in the Modern World, #74)

Individuals, families, and the various groups which make up the civil community, are aware of their inability to achieve a truly human life by their own unaided efforts; they see the need for a wider community where each one will make a specific contribution to an even broader implementation of the common good. For this reason they set up various forms of political communities. The political community, then, exists for the common good: this is its full justification and meaning and the source of its specific and basic right to exist. The common good embraces the sum total of all those conditions of social life which enable individuals, families, and organisations to achieve a complete and effective fulfilment.

The people who go to make up the political community are many and varied; quite rightly, then, they may have widely differing points of view. Therefore, lest the political community be jeopardised because all individuals follow their own opinion, an authority is needed to guide the energies of all toward the common good — not mechanically or despotically, but by acting above all as a moral force based on freedom and a sense of responsibility. It is clear that the political community and public authority are based on human nature, and therefore that they need to belong to an order established by God; nevertheless, the choice of the political regime and the appointment of rulers are left to the free decision of the citizens.

It follows that political authority, either within the political community as such or through organisations representing the state, must be exercised within the limits of the moral order and directed toward the common good, understood in the dynamic sense of the term, according to the juridical order legitimately established or due to be established. Citizens, then, are bound to obey. Accordingly, the responsibility, the status, and the importance of the rulers of the state are clear.

(The Church in the Modern World, #74)

4.   CANON LAW

Church law, known as canon law, is concerned with matters that govern the mission of the Church and the relationship of the faithful within the Catholic communion. Canon law includes the following:

- norms for celebrating the sacraments and public worship;

- norms for preaching;

- rules for the organisation of clerical and religious life;

- directives for Catholic education;

- directives for the use of Church properties and for the adjudication of conflicts;

- guidance for the allocation of penalties; and

- the articulation of the rights and obligations of the Christian faithful.

dispensation

Some laws may be dispensed by a proper authority, for a good reason. Other laws within the canons are considered unchangeable, because they are based upon divine revelation or upon natural law.

Some matters in canon law are purely disciplinary and may be subject to change; indeed many of the Church's disciplinary laws have changed in the course of history (think, for example, of the law that existed before Vatican II concerning Friday abstinence from meat). Some laws may be dispensed by a proper authority, for a good reason. Other laws within the canons are considered unchangeable, because they are based upon divine revelation or upon natural law.

universal laws

Canon law includes laws that are *universal*, laid down for everyone everywhere, and other laws that are *particular* – given for a particular territory, diocese or a given group of the faithful (for example, members of religious orders).

particular laws

The College of Bishops in union with the head of that college, the pope (or the pope himself as the head of the College of Bishops) is the supreme authority of the Church and the source of its universal laws. The universal laws for the Catholic Church are found in the *Code of Canon Law*, promulgated in 1983 in a postconciliar revised version (there is likewise a *Code of Canons of the Eastern Churches* (1990) for those oriental churches in communion with Rome).

Universal laws that are generated through the acts of ecumenical councils or the actions of the Roman Curia are usually promulgated in the official Vatican journal, *Acta Apostolicae Sedis*. Particular laws are those enacted for a certain territory or a given group of the faithful. Bishops enact particular laws that govern the celebration of the liturgy, the dates for Church feastdays and rules for fasting or common acts of penance in Lent, for example.

Church councils, both local and universal, have dealt not only with questions of doctrine, but also with matters of discipline, thus adding to the number of canons or norms in Church law. In addition, responses from the Holy See to questions raised by new or unforeseen situations also provide new legislation for the Church. Among the principles set down for the revision of the *Code of Canon Law* called for by Pope John XXIII at the time he convoked Vatican II (in 1959 ce) was that the law should be conceived of and used in a pastoral manner, that it be implemented according to the principle of subsidiarity (which means not having recourse to a higher level of authority unless one is unable to address questions properly at the lower level), and a concern to protect the rights of the faithful. The current *Code of Canon Law* follows most closely the theology and disciplinary initiatives of the Second Vatican Council.

4.1   THE AUTHORITY OF CANON LAW

Ecclesiastical laws and Church teachings are issued in forms that have significantly different levels of authority. The response of the faithful to Church teaching and Church norms should be correlated to the particular character of the teaching, according to who promulgates it and according to the type of document in which it is given. As Richard Gaillardetz, professor of Catholic Studies at the University of Toledo, Ohio, helpfully explains:

Ecclesiastical laws and Church teaching are issued in forms that have significantly different levels of authority.

Gaillardetz, Richard: *Teaching with Authority*, 1997, Collegeville, Liturgical Press, p.271.

What is at stake here is nothing less than a proper understanding of what constitutes Church membership and the fact that, in Catholic teaching, not all disagreement with ecclesiastical pronouncements necessarily separates one from the Roman Catholic communion. The following table is intended to help summarise the four categories of Church teaching and the response owed to each.

Level of Church teaching	Response of the faithful
Definitive dogma:	Assent of faith [the believer makes an act of faith, trusting that this teaching is revealed by God]
Definitive doctrine:	Firm acceptance [the believer 'accepts and holds' these teachings to be true]
Non-definitive, authoritative doctrine:	*Obsequium* of intellect and will [believer strives to assimilate a teaching of the Church into their religious stance, while recognising the remote possibility of Church error]
Prudential admonitions and provisional applications of Church doctrine:	Conscientious obedience [the believer obeys (the spirit of) any Church law or disciplinary action that does not lead to sin, even when questioning the ultimate value or wisdom of the law or action].

Here as elsewhere, the mature believer will respond with an autonomous conscience, receiving Church teaching as a call to personal faith and as an act of pastoral care on the part of Church leaders. Growth in faith, generosity and creative initiative, guided by the common good of the people of God, is meant to be the objective of Church law and to result in the freely-given obedience of the faithful.

5.   LAW IN THE SCRIPTURES

5.1   THE OLD TESTAMENT USE OF LAW

The Hebrew word *Torah* has a significance much richer than a strictly juridical understanding of 'law'. It means above all a 'teaching' given by God to human beings to guide their conduct. The term applies especially to the Old Testament tradition of teachings which is traditionally understood to have been given by Moses. As in the passage from Psalm 119 with which this chapter started, law in the Old Covenant signifies first of all an intimate relationship with God, sealed by a covenant in which the human partners commit themselves to follow the prescriptions set down by God in his revelation to Moses.

Law in the old Covenant signifies first of all an intimate relationship with God.

Much of Old Testament history is the story of a relationship between a faithful

God and a chosen people who kept falling into idolatry. The prophets were men and women completely given over to the word of God and inspired by the Spirit of God; their task was to call the chosen people back to a faithful observance, and they would repeatedly remind the people of their dignity as God's people and their need to be faithful witnesses to the values of the covenant.

In large segments of the Old Testament, one senses an almost adversarial relationship between God and his people, so strong is the railing of the prophets against the people's forgetfulness and idolatry. One of the greatest moments in the texts of the prophets is Jeremiah 31:33 where God promised to replace the laws engraved on stone (a reference to the tables of the Law given at Sinai) with a new law which would be written on the hearts of God's people – so that they would 'know God'.

The old Covenant never succeeded in establishing a lasting age of divine intimacy.

The law was incapable of saving God's chosen people.

Because their hearts would be changed such that they would listen to the inner message of the divine Spirit, God's people would finally obey all the prescriptions of the *Torah* spontaneously and freely. Throughout this back-and-forth relationship of covenant and failure, exile and return, idolatry and conversion, there is a repeated call to intimacy with God. But the Old Covenant never succeeded in establishing a lasting age of divine intimacy. In that sense, the Law was incapable of saving God's chosen people (as Paul saw in Romans 5:20).

5.2   THE NEW TESTAMENT USE OF LAW

In his Letter to the Galatians, Paul proclaimed a New Law (the Law of Christ; Gal 6-2); and the Letter to the Hebrews made a distinction between the Old Covenant and the New Covenant in Christ. The New Law would replace the Old.

In the Gospel of John, we find a dialectic which contrasts the law of the Jews (or the commandments of Old Covenant) with the commandments that Jesus himself had received from his Father and which lead to eternal life (Jn 12:49). Jesus received the commandment to give his life as a ransom for sinners, which is the greatest sign of love (Jn 15:13). This commandment was the sign of his Father's great love for him (Jn 10:17) and through him for the people. Likewise, Christians are obliged to keep the new commandments of God – to believe in Christ, to live in the truth and to witness to the love of God that they have received in Christ. Finally, Jesus summarises the New Law in his one commandment: 'love one another as I have loved you' (Jn13:34).

5.3   NEW REPLACES THE OLD

Biblical law remains always a polyphonic work, with several themes interacting in harmony one with another. For Christians, the following of Christ in self-sacrificing love is the major theme, with the commandments as a minor theme and as a symbol of God's authority. God's claim on our lives is accompanied by the New Testament understanding that the Old Law, after Jesus, no longer holds sway over our hearts and so is condemned according to its own norms (Jn 18:31; 19:7). A New Law has replaced the old, and it will remain forever the norm of the Christian life.

The Church, however, always retained a significant role for the Ten Commandments (as presented in Exod 20:2-17 and Deut 5:6-21). The Commandments are the guidelines for human conduct revealed to Moses and to Israel on Mount Sinai. Unlike any other part of the Hebrew Law, these commandments are described as having been spoken directly by God to the people of Israel, written directly in God's own hand on two tablets of stone. In the early Church, these commandments played an important role. St Augustine, in his pastoral catechesis, established a pattern of comparative relationships as follows:

- he related the theological virtue of faith to the creed and the sacraments;

- he related the virtue of hope to the Lord's prayer; and

- he related the virtue of charity to the fulfilment of the Ten Commandments.

The new *Catechism of the Catholic Church* published in 1992 continued this use of the Ten Commandments as the framework within which it conveys its moral teaching (see CCC #2052-2557).

The importance of the Ten Commandments in shaping moral catechesis through the centuries helps to explain how the Church produced generations of the lay faithful who lived very different religious lives. The Ten Commandments produced a spirit of 'boundary-defining' moral norms that established minimum requirements in the form of prohibitions – generally leaving any positive, goal-oriented expressions of moral virtue completely out of the picture. One of the breakthroughs of the Second Vatican Council was its move away from moral teaching rooted in prohibitions and commandments and towards a new moral teaching which makes an appeal to the creative freedom of the Christian faithful. The Ten Commandments need to be read by the Christian faithful as reminders of an agenda that demands insight and free improvisation in order to fully embody the faithfulness of God's people in every new age and situation.

One of the breakthroughs of the Second Vatican Council was its move away from moral teaching rooted in prohibitions and commandments and towards a new moral teaching which makes an appeal to the creative freedom of the Christian faithful.

Vatican II: *Pastoral Constitution on the Church in the Modern World*

Changes in Attitudes, Morals and Religion

A change in attitudes and structures frequently calls accepted values into question. This is above all true of young people who have grown impatient and, indeed, rebellious. Conscious of their own importance in society, they aspire to play a full part in it as soon as possible. Consequently, it frequently happens that parents and teachers find their tasks increasingly difficult.

Traditional institutions, laws and modes of thought and emotion do not always appear to be in harmony with today's world. This has given rise to a serious disruption of norms of behaviour.

The practice of religion is now happening in a completely new and open atmosphere. On the one hand people are taking a critical look at many magical world-views and prevailing superstitions and are turning instead to a more personal and active commitment to faith. Some have even developed a lively sense of the divine. On the other hand, greater numbers are falling away from the practice of religion altogether. In the past it was exceptional for someone to repudiate God and religion to the point of abandoning them; but nowadays it seems almost a matter-of-course to reject them as being incompatible with scientific knowledge and a new kind of humanism. It is not only in philosophy that such trends are expressed, there are signs of them in literature, art, the humanities, the interpretation of history and even civil law – all of which is very disturbing to many people.

(See: Pastoral Constitution on the Church in the Modern World #7)

6.   THE SOURCE OF ALL LAW

In his teaching about different types of law, Thomas Aquinas (1225-1274 ce) named the Eternal Law first, showing that this is the source from which all other law arises. In doing so, he was following a long tradition of Christian thought transmitted by St Augustine who himself was handing on the ideas of the Greek stoic philosophers of the third century bce and of Cicero (a Roman author, orator, and politician; 106-43 bce). In this way of seeing things, the idea of law is analogical (meaning something significantly different in different contexts). In this way Aquinas was able to include under the idea of law both the sovereignty of divine providence as well as the most contingent ordinances of the civil legislation. Because God is the end or goal of human destiny and the source of eternal happiness, all law leads to God. God is the objective, and therefore law links human powers and human activity with the object that fulfills all their potentiality.

God himself can be considered the supreme law, identified with divine Wisdom and with the providence which governs the whole created universe: this law is eternal and universal. It is also mysterious and hidden to our eyes, being identical with God's own reality. Against this background, we can understand the way in which Aquinas in his *Summa Theologiae* describes the eternal law:

> Through his wisdom God is the founder of the universe of things, and we have said that in relation to them he is like an artist with regard to the things he makes. We have also said that he is the governor of all acts and motions to be found in each and every creature. And so, as being the principle through which the universe is created, *divine wisdom* means *art*, or *exemplar*, or *idea*, and likewise it also means *law*, as moving all things to their due ends. Accordingly the eternal law is nothing other than the exemplar of divine wisdom as directing the motions and acts of everything. (ST IaIIae, 93,1)

In human beings – endowed with reason and having a spiritual destiny – the eternal law is participated in, in a special fashion. It follows from the idea of the eternal law that every single being should follow a providence characteristic of its nature. Given the nature of human beings to become themselves a kind of practical providence in the created order, divine providence delegates to humans a level of insight rooted in human reason and human freedom which is called, in the language of a the theological tradition, 'the natural law'. An entire section of this course will be devoted to a discussion of the natural law, both because it is so badly misunderstood in our day and because it is so important to the Catholic moral tradition. For that reason, natural law will not be treated further in this section which is devoted primarily to an understanding of how positive law needs to be interpreted as a pedagogy of freedom.

EXERCISE 2:

The idea of law has very different layers of meaning. One of the key ideas in the Catholic theology of law is the understanding that all norms are but a part of the complex relationship between 'divine norming' and 'human normed' – strange language, of course, but language that nonetheless points towards the truth that God's idea of reality stands behind all human ideas of what's right and what's wrong. Think, then, for a minute about how God's idea of reality – what we call here eternal law – is always present as the background which gives meaning to every particular instance of law.

The idea of law is analogical meaning something significantly different in different contexts.

Aquinas was able to include under the idea of law both the sovereignty of divine providence as well as the most contingent ordinances of the civil legislation.

a) Think of any simple instance where there is an easy link between positive law and the eternal law. Perhaps it will be something to do with your vocation in life. Positive law demands certain requirements linked to marriage, religious life, holy orders or ministerial service in the Church; and you, moved by the conviction that God is calling you to this state in life, willingly accept the legislated norms as representing God's own will. What is there of the help, comfort and joy in this idea? Write 5 lines.

b) By contrast, think of an experience where the demands of positive law have been painfully difficult. Perhaps it will be something to do with your frustration at a difference of opinion or even of vision with the Church. How does the idea that this positive law, as a culturally conditioned (perhaps fallible) expression of the eternal law help you to understand your responsibility to conform, and to deal with your feelings about the matter? Write 5 lines.

c) What more do you need to know about the meaning of law in the context of morality? Write down your questions and your areas of confusion, and try to resolve them.

7. AUTHORITY AND GRACE

7.1 TWO VERSIONS OF MORAL RESPONSIBILITY

A very legalistic version of morality has held sway for so long – both in Church and in society – that the re-introduction of a classical account of moral responsibility (especially the account given by Aquinas) appears to some to be an innovation in our days. The *Catechism of the Catholic Church* gives us an important positive example of this shift from a legalistic moral framework founded upon authority to a new framework of prophetic responsibility founded upon grace. Here is the introduction by the Catechism to the treatment of morality:

> The dignity of the human person is rooted in the image and likeness of God; it is fulfilled in his vocation to divine beatitude. It is essential to a human being freely to direct himself to this fulfilment. (CCC #1700)

The goal of the paragraphs that follow is to explain this morality of prophetic responsibility and to show the difference between a moral system based on authority and one based on grace. However, in order to do that, it will be necessary to develop a contrast (unfortunately a rather complicated one) between these two rival systems.

Contemporary civil law and jurisprudence are rooted in positive law, seeing such law as absolute in itself (not as merely one piece of a vast analogical structure). There is little personal encouragement to be found in popular culture for an understanding of discernment and the personal judgments that are integral to a system of graced morality. Most legal systems of modern Western nations are the product of the same shift in thinking (which will be examined soon) that led to the abandonment of a Christian morality of grace and discernment.

The renewal of Catholic theology since the Second Vatican Council has emphasised a number of theological points that can help one to grasp the sense of a morality of grace. Think of the Council's teaching about the universal call to holiness (*Dogmatic Constitution on the Church* #40), or its teaching on the apostolic overflow of the witness to Christian values in the marketplace (*Church* #33-34) or the doctrine of the common priesthood of all the faithful (*Church* #10,34). These teachings, as well as many others from the Council, presuppose a return to a morality of discernment rooted in a clear understanding of human intentionality (the concept of 'intentionality' will be explained soon) and a

There has been a shift from a legalistic moral framework founded upon authority to a new framework of prophetic responsibility founded upon grace.

theology of grace. For the moment, it suffices to say that the present discussion of the nature and role of law in the Christian life has important implications for our sense of meaning and for our happiness.

7.2   THE HUMAN PERSONALITY

In continuity with the ideas of the classical moral philosophers and of the majority of the Fathers of the Church, Aquinas had a dynamic and creative understanding of the human personality. Human powers (intelligence, senses etc.) are also potencies – in the sense that they are ordered to find their fulfilment by reaching out to objects that complete the person and enrich him or her (the term 'potency' here means a certain potential, together with the inclination towards its fulfilment). Such a sense of humanity recognises the importance of intentionality. Intentionality means roughly the same thing as 'aiming' our energies at the proper target, and reaching out (by discernment, by desire and by choosing) to become united with what is good for us.

potencies

intentionality

Each person possesses five external senses and sense appetites, together with the internal senses of memory and imagination and their corresponding appetites, and a rational and spiritual intellect with its corresponding appetite known as the will.

senses

sense appetites

rational intellect

spiritual intellect

will

Each one of the powers listed above has a natural orientation to its proper good which in practice means that it has an attraction towards what properly satisfies its craving. The most fundamental power (also called a 'passion') is love, aroused by the attraction of what is good. The life of intentionality, therefore, means that a human being's moral life is always dynamic, always reaching out, always being drawn to its fulfilment.

Naturally, since human beings begin their lives as helpless infants, it takes both physical development and some training in discernment, taste and refinement to establish a proper orientation of these faculties towards their objects. Human education entails shaping the sensibilities of the young by teaching the commandments, handing on the customs of the family and the community, and teaching the skills which will facilitate these good results. All of this involves the development of physical coordination, training in virtue, social skills and cooperation as well as the habitual orientation of the senses and the mind to beauty and truth.

faculties

= powers

= passions

The proper integration of human powers and social objects leads to a life of virtue. In this understanding, virtue never means just a list of socially-approved qualities, but rather the graceful results of growth and intelligence. Virtue means arriving at a balanced appreciation of the relative weight of competing appetites, the skill (based on experience) of controlling one's impulses for the sake of a greater good, a certain creativity of expression and a perspective rooted in the common good of the community (a whole unit will be devoted to the idea of virtue and its importance for the Christian moral life).

According to Aristotle and Aquinas, it is virtue which makes any human act good, and also makes the person who acts good.

The authentic meaning of freedom has already been explained as the maximisation of understanding and willingness. What was earlier called autonomous behaviour can be seen here in its fuller development as the life of virtue. In the formula crafted by Aristotle and adopted by Aquinas, virtue makes any human act good, and also makes the person who acts good. When looked at within this context, it is easy to see the role of law as a pedagogy of freedom, pointing us in the direction of the true human good so as to instill good habits of reaching out toward what is really good for us. This pedagogy prepares a person for improvising excellent behaviour that will enhance that person's attachment to goodness. In this account, the law exists for the sake of freedom, not vice versa.

7.3 OCKHAM'S NOMINALISM

Towards the middle of the fourteenth century, a Franciscan philosopher and theologian named William of Ockham began to attract attention with his writings, which ultimately became a milestone in the intellectual history of the Middle Ages and the source of a movement which has come to be known as *nominalism*. Only some key points that characterise Ockham's moral thinking will be sketched here, but they will suffice to demonstrate the huge difference which separates him from the tradition we have just described.

nominalism

Ockham postulated freedom as *a given*, as a necessary characteristic of human experience. For him, freedom was the power that humans possess at all times to make the choice for one or other of two contradictory positions. Freedom is therefore a state of complete indetermination or indifference. No natural inclination draws human powers towards objects as their proper ends. Ockham refused to admit any natural inclination in the will towards what is good or towards human happiness. Following his notion of freedom, people can easily turn away from their ultimate good and from happiness. Likewise God, as the ultimate authority, exercises a sovereignty over human beings which is completely arbitrary. Ockham thought that God could command people to hate him.

Ockham refused to admit any natural inclination in the will towards what is good or toward human happiness.

In so conceiving the moral life, Ockham destroyed the fundamental link that St Thomas had established between the human spirit and God. Where Aquinas recognised the love of the human heart for God as the natural human desire for happiness (humankind's final good), Ockham replaced that ancient understanding with the necessary relationship of freedom to precepts. As a result, the central notion of a nominalist morality is obligation. In consequence, moral theology from the late Middle Ages up to the modern period no longer studied the quest for happiness (Aquinas's starting point) as the first step in moral teaching; it failed to identify the good towards which the free person is drawn. Rather, with Ockham, it is the law (or the precepts of some divine or human authority) that becomes the first and fundamental reality of any moral system.

Ockham replaced the ancient understanding of a desire for happiness with the necessary relationship of freedom to precepts. As a result, the central notion of a nominalist morality is obligation.

In Ockham's approach, the concept of 'duty' becomes the preoccupation of all moral reasoning. Good acts are reduced to questions of obedience. Any act that is not commanded by the precept of an authority is considered to be indifferent, without moral significance. This represents a radical transformation of moral understanding. Among other consequences, it isolates individual choices from any historical or moral development of the individual or from any assessment of the fittingness of what is appropriate in a particular community.

duty

Ockham's view, and those based upon it, has been dominant for some centuries, but today things are swinging back to the more ancient view.

Extract from Servais Pinckaers: *Morality: The Catholic View*

St Thomas had argued that free choice proceeded from both reason and will. It was thus a power to choose derived from our two spiritual faculties and quickened by the inclinations to truth, goodness and happiness that animate these faculties. Hence, one can call it a freedom for excellence or perfection. It is the power to engage in excellent actions, actions that are both true and the good, even though the agent may in fact fail and do evil.

Ockham squarely reverses the relationship: free choice does not proceed from reason and will; instead, it precedes them on the level of action, for we can choose to think or not to think, to will or not to will. Hence, free choice is the first faculty of the human person, whose act does not originally depend on anything but his or her own choice. It will be defined as the power to choose indifferently between contraries, between yes and no, good and evil. Hence, it is rightly described as a freedom of indifference.

A veritable revolution is occurring here in the conception of the human person and of human action. This revolution begins by breaking away from spiritual nature and its inclinations, especially its inclination to happiness. Ockham affirms that the human person can choose indifferently between being happy and not being happy, as well as between preserving or not preserving his existence. Nature is no longer the source of freedom; it is henceforth subordinated to choice, being below and external to it. The famous maxim of the Ancients, sequi naturam (follow nature) loses its meaning; instead, a new vision emerges: dominari naturam. The ideal becomes the domination and enslavement of nature.

(Pinckaers, Servais: *Morality: The Catholic View*, 2001, South Bend Indiana, St Augustine's Press, pp.68-69)

7.4   TWO CONCEPTS OF CONSCIENCE

Under the influence of Ockham, the study of conscience took on a greater importance than it had played in the theology of St Thomas. Within the moral teaching influenced by nominalism, it is conscience which stands between law and freedom; it applies law to specific acts and judges these acts in the name of the law or precept. That is why, for this tradition, the principal task of the moralist is to resolve cases of conscience. Conscience in this sense looks exclusively to follow laws and, given Ockham's understanding of morality, tries to find ways in which the law does not bind (so that the person may have a greater range of freedom).

Within the moral teaching influenced by nominalism, it is conscience which stands between law and freedom.

For Aquinas, on the other hand, conscience exercises a richer function than merely imposing legal obligations. Conscience signifies the voice of God that resounds in the human heart (Cardinal Newman once referred to conscience as the voice of Christ). To speak of conscience in the tradition of Ockham is to evoke a climate of heteronomy – yielding to constraints of the law that often make no spontaneous internal sense to the person. To speak of conscience in the tradition of grace and virtue is to evoke the climate of autonomy – taking ultimate responsibility to synthesise our senses, the guidance of the commandments, the traditions of the Church and the constraints and possibilities of our unique circumstances. As the *Catechism* says so well:

> When he listens to his conscience, the prudent man can hear God speaking. (CCC #1775)

The Church teaches that a person must have a well-informed conscience. The Catechism has a helpful description of what this means in practice:

> Conscience must be informed and moral judgment enlightened. A well-formed conscience is upright and truthful. It formulates its judgments according to reason, in conformity with the true good willed by the wisdom of the creator ... The education of the conscience is a life-long

task. From the earliest years, it awakens the child to the knowledge and practice of the interior law recognised by conscience. Prudent education teaches virtue; it prevents or cures fear, selfishness and pride, resentment arising from guilt, and feelings of complacency born of human weakness and faults. The education of the conscience guarantees freedom and engenders peace of heart. (CCC §1783-4)

Thousands of books have been published on law, conscience and obligation. Our goal here has not been to summarise that vast literature but rather to present an understanding of how a healthy view of law fosters human autonomy. In the tradition of Aquinas, all law is for the sake of freedom. Unfortunately, we live in a society deeply influenced by the ideas of Ockham who proposed that all freedom is for the sake of law.

In the sections that follow, especially in the study of St Thomas's theology of the New Law of grace, it will become clear how the position taken here fits into the whole structure of moral teaching. A choice must be made between the path of grace or the path of authority. The path of grace has as its goal the supernatural dignity of a Christian transformed by a new life in Christ and guided by God's own spirit. The path of authority is preoccupied with self-justification under the burden of law and seeks excuses and ways to escape from that burden.

The path of grace has as its goal the supernatural dignity of a Christian transformed by a new life in Christ and guided by God's own spirit. The path of authority is preoccupied with self-justification under the burden of law and seeks excuses and ways to escape from that burden.

Fig. 6: *John Henry Cardinal Newman*

John Henry Cardinal Newman

Conscience is a law of the mind; yet [Christians] would not grant that it is nothing more; I mean that it was not a dictate, nor conveyed the notion of responsibility, of duty, of a threat and a promise ... [Conscience] is a messenger of him, who, both in nature and in grace, speaks to us behind a veil, and teaches and rules us by his representatives. Conscience is the aboriginal Vicar of Christ.

(Newman, Henry, in CCC #1778)

EXERCISE 3:

a) *Contrast the two approaches to conscience as understood by Ockham and Aquinas. Write 10 lines.*

SECTION TWO
NATURAL LAW

I.   HOW WE KNOW MORAL TRUTH

In an earlier section, it was explained how morality is a search for happiness. There are a number of ways in which persons can know where to look for happiness. There is Scripture and revelation. In God's word, and especially in the person of Jesus who is the Word of God incarnate, we find clues to the earthly and eternal happiness that God promises us. Protestant theologies mostly limit God's revelation to the word of Scripture and the person of Jesus. The Catholic tradition, however, believes that God's plan for us and God's view of human happiness is mediated not only through Scripture and revelation but also through our reasonable reflection on human experience and the created world. This mediated understanding of God's plan is known as natural law. Many Church documents refer to the fact that our moral teachings are based on the norms of human nature; for example *Gaudium et Spes* (#51), which speaks of objective standards 'based on the nature of the person and his acts'.

The Catholic tradition, however, believes that God's plan for us and God's view of human happiness is mediated not only through Scripture and revelation but also through our reasonable reflection on human experience and the created world.

Natural law tends to have a bad reputation; it is sometimes confused with the 'laws of nature' which govern animal behaviour and contain the laws of physics and other scientific facts. At other times it is associated solely with sexual morality or is seen as being static, inflexible, medieval or even legalistic.

Natural law refers to nature, but only to human, rational nature.

In fact, it would be accurate to say that natural law is neither 'natural' in the sense of having to do with animal nature; nor is it truly law. Natural law does refer to nature, but only to human, rational nature. It is called 'law' only in a specific sense; it does set forth norms for moral behaviour, but not in the same way as the laws of Ireland or of the United States.

It is more accurate to say that natural law is a process than a proposition; it describes the way in which we come to know God's will through the use of reason. It is so important that nearly all Catholic moral teachings are derived from it. Because in principle it is a kind of moral knowing that is available to all people, regardless of their religious faith, it might better be described as 'common human morality'. It provides a bridge between believers and non-believers who all have equal access to morality by means of natural law.

2.   THE ORIGIN OF NATURAL LAW

2.1   SCRIPTURAL ORIGINS

For Christians, the origin of natural law is unremarkable. It is referred to by St Paul in his letter to the Romans where he observed that there were Gentiles who, without benefit of the Jewish law or the prophets, still seemed to be living upright lives. He wrote:

> When the Gentiles who do not have the [religious] law, do by nature [Greek: *nomon physei*] those things which are of the law, they are a law unto themselves ... they show the work of the law *in their hearts*, their conscience bearing witness to them ... (Rom 2:14-15)

Natural law was known to Greek and Roman philosophers, and it is likely that St Paul borrowed his insights about the gentiles from Stoic philosophy. Paul does not suggest that this 'natural knowledge' of the law is incompatible with the Gospel, only that it is another way of discovering the same truth, at least in moral matters.

Paul does not suggest that this 'natural knowledge' of the law is incompatible with the Gospel, only that it is another way of discovering the same truth, at least in moral matters.

Despite these simple beginnings, by the thirteenth century the idea of natural law had become complicated and controversial.[1] Thomas Aquinas inherited dozens of definitions of natural law, some of which were irreconcilable with others. So he and other medieval writers set out to clarify this tradition and to make it more compatible with Christian morality. In the end, natural law would rival the Gospels themselves in its influence upon the development of Christian moral norms. A quick review of the history of natural law will show us how St Thomas and others distilled the tradition they received and how the idea has gone on developing right up to the contemporary period.

2.2   NATURAL LAW HISTORY: THE GREEKS & ROMANS

Pre-Socratic philosophers and playwrights also invoked some idea of the natural law. In his play *Antigone*, Aeschylus (525-456 bce) invoked a form of natural law as the idea of 'unwritten statutes of heaven'. The character, Antigone, claimed that this unwritten law allowed her to ignore civil authorities and bury her brother against the will of the state. The philosopher Demosthenes (384-322 bce) described what he called 'the law for all men given by nature'. These early writers saw natural law as both above and before any civil law.

Plato (427-347 bce) talked about an 'idea of justice' that was supramundane, in the heavens, and reflected only faintly in practical human affairs. His student Aristotle (384-322 bce), on the other hand, saw the world around us as real. The difference in their views is summarised by the theologian, John Mahoney.

---

1   A detailed history of the development of natural law is found in Michael Crowe's, *The Changing Profile of the Natural Law*, 1977, The Hague, Nijhoff.

John Mahoney: *Making of Moral Theology*

Aristotle shared with his master [Plato] the view that written laws are too universal in their formulation and scope to cover all possible contingencies and eventualities, and he explained that any lawmaker must confine himself only to what happens in the great majority of cases and legislate for them. But Aristotle differs from Plato in his view of exceptional cases and emergencies. For Plato, the exception is a deviation and deficiency, due to the imperfect way in which worldly reality embodies and represents the ideal; whereas for Aristotle, the exception, far from weakening the law, actually improves and corrects it.

For Aristotle it is the law itself which is inherently weak and imperfect, precisely because it is universal and general in its formulations. Worldly reality is too rich and varied to be comprehended by a general law, with the result that on occasion the general law has to be corrected and improved in order to bring it in line with real life. This correction and improvement of the law in a minority of cases is done simply by the individual's ignoring what the law says, and by his contravening the letter of the law in order to observe the spirit, and above all the true purpose of the law. What defect there is [in the law] is to be found not in concrete reality, as Plato held, but in the positive law which is too abstract and indeterminate.

(Mahoney, John: *Making of Moral Theology*, 1987, New York, Oxford, pp.35-37)

Later on, the great Roman orator Cicero (106-43 bce) stressed the *universality* and *immutability* of natural law:

> There is a true law, right reason, agreeable to nature, known to all men, constant and eternal, which calls to duty by its precepts, deters from evil by its prohibitions. This law cannot be departed from without guilt … Neither can the senate or the people loose us from this law. Nor is there one law at Rome and another at Athens … but the same law, unchanging, and eternal, binds all races of men and all times …
>
> (Cicero: De Rep III, 22 (PL 6:660-661); cited in Crowe, *Changing Profile*, p.237)

The second-century Roman lawyer, Ulpian (172-228 ce), described natural law as that which 'nature has taught all animals [Latin: *Lex natura est quod natura docuit omnia animalia*]. For this law is not proper to man but is common to all animals, whether born on land or in the sea, and birds also.'

Ulpian's unnuanced definition would contribute to profound confusion about the relationship between animal and human behaviour.

Because Ulpian was widely respected as an authority by medieval writers, his definition was assured a place in medieval moral theology, but it also created a false connection between animal and human behaviour. Ulpian's unnuanced definition would contribute to profound confusion about the relationship between animal and human behaviour. Even today, it is not uncommon to hear people assess human behaviour – usually in the sexual realm – by comparing it to (presumed) animal behaviour.

In the ninth century ce, Isidore of Seville took a more political approach and said that 'natural law was that which is common to all nations and set up by a natural instinct and not given by any positive institution'. Two centuries later, in 1160 ce, the canon lawyer, Gratian, further confused matters with his definition of natural law as 'that which is contained in the law and the Gospel'. This gave the impression that natural law was in some way religious or faith-based, which in fact is precisely what it is not.

2.3   NATURAL LAW HISTORY: THE MIDDLE AGES

When William of Auxerre (a contemporary of Thomas Aquinas) wrote his *Summa Aurea* in about 1220 ce, he distinguished several senses or levels of natural law.

The wide sense is 'what nature has taught all animals'; the narrow sense is 'that which connects the natural law with natural reason which is almost intuitive'. Elsewhere he adds a third sense, the widest of all, in which the natural law is synonymous with the harmony of creation.[2]

These definitions are a representative sample. They suggest the wide range of views of natural law that existed by the time Thomas Aquinas appeared on the scene in the early thirteenth century. In his earlier writings, Thomas talked about natural law as something impressed on human nature, which had to do with animal functions as well as rational ones.[3] In his later writings, however, he moved away from seeing natural law as something common to all animals and narrowed his focus to an essentially rational view of natural law. Natural law was a *rational participation* in the eternal law; as such, it pertained only to human beings. The clearest statement of his thought is found in the *Summa*. The most important passage is as follows.

Thomas Aquinas: *Summa Theologia*

It is evident that all things partake somewhat of the Eternal Law, inasmuch as they derive their respective inclinations to their proper ends and acts, and it is imprinted on them.

But among all others, the rational creature is subject to divine providence in the most excellent way, insofar as it partakes of providence by being provident both for itself and for others. Wherefore it has a share of the eternal reason, whereby it has a natural inclination to its proper act and end. And this participation of the eternal law in the rational creature is called the natural law.

Even irrational animals partake in their own way of the eternal reason, just as the rational creature does; but because the rational creature partakes thereof in an intellectual and rational manner, the irrational creatures' participation is not properly called a law, since a law is something pertaining to reason. Irrational creatures do not partake of it except by similitude.

(ST, 1a2ae, q.91, a.2, and ad.3)

Shortly after this, Thomas distinguished three kinds of natural law: that which is common to all beings, that which is common to all animals, and that which is common to rational persons alone (ST 1a2ae, q.94, a.2).

It is clear from this passage that Thomas viewed natural law primarily as a function of reason, and is therefore proper only to persons. It is through reason that we participate in the eternal law; this means that God's will is not imposed on us from without, but that we are invited into it, to know it and to understand it.

The language of 'participation' that Thomas uses is marvellously dynamic and powerful. It suggests that natural law is not just a proposition or a static order, but an evolving discovery of God's plan through reasonable reflection on creation. It gives us, as rational creatures, a certain privilege and autonomy. It is also interesting to note that one of the characteristics of natural law as it applies to persons is its social character; it enables persons to provide not only for themselves – as a fish might know how to feed itself – but for others as well.

Even though animals and other created things partake of the natural law 'in their own way', they do so irrationally and without understanding; only humans

In his later writings, Aquinas moved away from seeing the natural law as something common to all animals, and narrowed his focus to an essentially rational view of natural law.

Natural law is a rational participation in the eternal law; as such, it pertained only to human beings.

God's will is not imposed on us from without; we are invited into it, to know it and to understand it.

UNIT TWO
SECTION TWO

---

2.   William of Auxerre, *Summa Aurea*, translation in Crowe, *The Changing Profile of the Natural Law*, p.116.

3.   See, St Thomas: *Commentary on the Sentences of Peter Lombard* (this was a standard textbook in the early middle ages), *In 4 Sent.* d.33, q.1, a.1: 'Natural law is nothing other than the concept naturally impressed on man which directs him to acting properly toward his end, whether toward things of his generic nature, i.e., generation, eating, and things like that, or things having to do with his rational nature'.

The Thomistic understanding of natural law as a dynamic participation in the Eternal Law that is proper to rational creatures has became the bedrock of Catholic moral theology.

participate in it in this most excellent way. This Thomistic understanding of natural law as a dynamic participation in the Eternal Law that is proper to rational creatures has became the bedrock of Catholic moral theology as can be seen from the passage below from the *Catechism of the Catholic Church*:

> Man participates in the wisdom and goodness of the Creator who gives him mastery over his acts and the ability to govern himself with a view to the true and the good. The natural law expresses the original moral sense which enables man to discern by reason the good and the evil, the truth and the lie.

> (*Catechism of the Catholic Church*, Chapter 4, #1954)

2.4   NATURAL LAW FROM THE HEART

Even though natural law is proper to rational creatures, it is not known in a narrowly rational way like mathematical truth. St Paul described the Gentiles as having this law 'in their hearts'. William of Auxerre described it as 'almost intuitive'. And Aquinas described it as an inclination towards our proper end. So it is clear that apprehension of the natural law involves a unique kind of knowing. The French philosopher Jacques Maritain (1882-1973 ce) describes this awareness of natural law as *connatural*, or embedded in our natures:

> The genuine concept of natural law is the concept of law which is natural not only insofar as it expresses the normality of functioning of human nature, but also insofar as it is naturally known, i.e., through inclination or through *connaturality*, not through conceptual knowledge and by way of reasoning. The judgments in which natural law is made manifest to practical reason do not proceed from any conceptual, discursive or rational exercise of reason [but from] that connaturality or congeniality through which what is consonant with essential inclinations of human nature is grasped by the intellect as good, what is dissonant, bad.

> (Maritain, Jacques: 'On Knowledge through Connaturality', in *Range of Reason*, 1952, New York, Scribner, pp.26-7)

This is not to suggest that natural law is irrational, but that it is deeper than just rational judgments. It is analogous to the internal 'knowledge' that an acorn has which allows it to grow into an oak rather than into a mulberry bush. Because it is connatural, this knowledge is not alien or external to us; it is not to be looked on as knowledge that we know or acquire, but as knowledge that we have, planted deep within us by God's providence.

3.   DOES NATURAL LAW CHANGE?

3.1   STATIC OR EVOLVING?

Natural law is based upon the assumption that human nature is something quite special. This provides an objective base for natural law. However, human nature is not static or abstract. As Irish moral theologian Enda McDonagh says, it may be tempting to think we can discover a pure and simple version of human nature, abstract from the messy details of human life, but because we are social creatures who are affected by the world around us, an adequate understanding of human nature must take these influences into account:

> The reasonableness [of Christian ethics] is more closely conditioned by some other general features … The first of these is a sense of the reality and recognisability of the human, independently of sin and grace… It is from this base that one derives the universal principles of natural law morality … But if either reason or human reality and possibility are abstracted from their ambiguous history with all the psychological and social conditions and limitations, the abstracted reason and humanity are bound to prove misleading.

(McDonagh, Enda: *The Making of Disciples*, 1982, Wilmington, Delaware, Glazier, p.33)

Richard Gula of the Franciscan School of Theology, Berkeley, USA makes a similar point about the meaning of 'natural':

> Natural is not opposed to artificial, nor does it refer to the well-defined given structures and functions of the body or of any created reality … rather natural … is shorthand for the total complexity of human reality taken in all its relationships and with all its potential.

(Gula, Richard: *Reason Informed by Faith*, 1989, New York, Paulist Press, p.238)

It would not be proper to say that natural law changes, as if God 'changed his mind' about the nature and purpose of creation. We believe that God has a plan for creation and that it is clear and final, but our *experience* of that plan and our *knowledge of it* is not complete. Consider, for example, the recent discovery of the human genome. This is entirely new knowledge for us; Plato, Aristotle, Aquinas and all the rest of them had no idea there was such a thing, let alone that it could be described in such detail. Is this fact not significant for how we understand 'human nature'? How will this unprecedented discovery affect our own self-understanding and our awareness of God's plan in our lives?

Or what about the differences between men and women that have been described and scientifically documented? If natural law is a process of reasonable reflection upon human nature, then we must ask 'Whose nature?' – men's nature or women's nature? If we are to consider the human person fully and adequately, theologians must take a much more serious look at both men's and women's experience so as to expand and correct the biases of an excessively male perspective. This is particularly important in the area of sexual morality because all evidence shows that women's experience of sexuality is far different from men's. Surely these differences are more than skin deep and so must have some important implications for our understanding of human nature, and of natural law. Marie Vianney Bilgrien, project director at the Tepeyac Institute of the Diocese of El Paso, Texas, summarises the importance of taking women's experience more seriously:

> Until now, men's experience has been accepted almost exclusively as the norm for the human person. Because women's experience has been left out, feminists claim that something distinctly human, not just something feminine, has been left out. Androcentrism distorts both human experience and theology. Both need to be corrected. The issue raised by feminists should concern us all, because it is a call to be truthful and faithful to God's revelation. It cuts much deeper than equality, power, inclusiveness and freedom. It affects how we know God and therefore how we relate to God.

(Bilgrien, Marie Vianney: 'The Voices of Women in Moral Theology', in *America*, 173 no.20, p.14)

EXERCISE 5:

a) *What is the relationship between human experience and natural law? Are they the same? Write 5 lines.*

b) *How can we be sure that our experience is authentic and a reliable mediation of God's will? Write 5 lines.*

4. IMPLICATIONS OF NATURAL LAW

Having sketched the history and the theological implications of natural law in Catholic tradition, one might now ask: 'So what?' What difference does it make in practical moral decision-making? Examples from three areas of morality will show us evidence of natural law thinking – sexual morality, health-care ethics, and social ethics.

4.1 SEXUAL ETHICS AND NATURAL LAW

Perhaps nowhere is the natural law basis of Catholic morality more apparent than in sexual ethics. Although scripture does provide some moral norms, scripture is far richer and more useful in the area of motivation and discipleship. Scripture tells us not so much what we ought or ought not to do, but how we ought to do it. To this end, one might think of the scriptural prohibition of fornication and marital infidelity that are found in both the Hebrew and Christian Scriptures. The real rationale and explanation of these norms, however, is found not in Scripture but in moral reasoning based on a certain understanding of the human person.

- The primary norm is our understanding of the unity of the person. Although we have various capacities and abilities, moral maturity involves integrating all these capacities and abilities so that we become single-minded and at peace.

- A second norm is that our bodies (and created matter in general) are not only good, but are even capable of mediating grace.

4.2 NATURAL LAW AND HEALTH-CARE

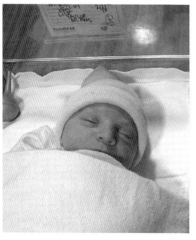

A second area rooted in natural law is health-care ethics. While Catholic ethicists may differ from others on some points, they are readily able to converse with those who do not share their faith. They do this by means of natural law arguments based on certain presuppositions about the human person. In questions about allocation of health-care resources, for example, they draw on the principle of distributive justice tempered by the Gospel command to serve the poor; in debates about treatment choices, they turn to the proper calculation of burdens and benefits in order to determine which treatments should be considered 'ordinary' (i.e., morally obligatory) and which are 'extraordinary' (i.e., those whose burdens appear to outweigh the benefits and which are therefore morally optional).

Any individual patient's discernment about treatment options is clearly aided by faith and by the theological virtue of hope, but it is rooted also in concrete and specific deliberations about prognosis and outcomes. The principle of informed consent, which is of primary importance in making health-care decisions, is based not so much on Scripture as on basic assumptions about moral agency and the right to understand and agree to anything that is done to the patient.

The principle of informed consent is based not so much on Scripture as on basic assumptions about moral agency and the right to understand and agree to anything that is done to the patient.

4.3   SOCIAL ETHICS

Politics is the art or virtue of living together in the *polis*, or city (we would understand this today as society, whether urban or not). It is the public aspect of ethics and morality. The goal of politics is not personal perfection but the common good which enables us to pursue personal perfection or virtue.

Even though Catholics understand the *polis*, or city, as a symbol of the 'heavenly Jerusalem', the rules which need to be developed to live together are largely based on natural law. These rules focus on fairness, truth, equitable distribution of goods, public safety and individual contributions to the whole. While people of goodwill might disagree on the best way to achieve these things, every rational person would agree that no society can exist without them.

The importance of natural law can be seen whenever the Church speaks publicly on some social issue. When the Church addresses moral issues in economics, foreign policy, human rights or health-care she does so on the basis of natural law, presenting arguments that can be considered and appropriated by everyone, not just Roman Catholics. Church documents often refer explicitly to the basis of its teachings, as can be seen from this passage from John Paul II's 1981 encyclical *Laborem Exercens* in which he notes the human reality of work and the fact that work brings perfection to human nature:

> The Church considers it her task always to call attention to the dignity and rights of those who work … and to help to … guide changes so as to ensure authentic progress by man and society.

(John Paul II: 1981, *Laborem Exercens*, #1)

Elsewhere he notes,

> through work, man not only transforms nature, adapting it to his own needs, but also achieves fulfilment as a human being and indeed in a sense becomes 'more of a human being'.

(John Paul II: 1981, *Laborem Exercens*, #2)

5.   NATURAL LAW AND REVELATION

5.1   OPEN TO ALL

We have already noted that even though St Paul was aware of moral discernment among those who had neither the Law nor the Prophets, he did not consider this kind of morality to be at odds with the moral teaching of Judaism nor that of the Gospels. Indeed, many of the household codes (e.g., Col 3:18-4:1; Eph 5:21-6:4;) and catalogues of vices (for example, Gal 5:16-26 and 1 Cor 6:9:10) which he uses in his letters are very similar to those found in Stoic philosophy which had no religious base at all. His concern was not whether or not the Gentiles had this law (he clearly assumes they did); his concern was how they came to know it.

The *Catechism of the Catholic Church* defines the natural law in these terms:

UNIT TWO
SECTION TWO

The natural law states the first and essential precepts which govern the moral life. It hinges upon the desire for God and submission to him, who is the source and judge of all that is good, as well as upon the sense the other is one's equal. Its principal precepts are expressed in the Decalogue. It is called *natural* not in reference to the nature of irrational beings, but because reason which decrees it properly belongs to human nature. It provides the indispensable moral foundation for building the human community. Finally, it provides the necessary basis for the civil law. The natural law provides revealed law and grace with a foundation prepared by God and in accordance with the Spirit.

(*Catechism of the Catholic Church*, ##1955,1959,1960)

This description reflects much of what has already been discussed, but it also indicates that the principal precepts of natural law are found in the Decalogue (especially from the fourth to the tenth commandments). It is true that these represent the most basic rules of human conduct, and that they are found in some form in virtually every known culture. The Catechism's description also makes an important theological affirmation, viz., 'natural law provides revealed law and grace with a foundation ...' This is another way of stating the axiom 'grace perfects nature'.

5.2 NATURAL FOUNDATION FOR GRACE

Catholics believe that human nature, even though wounded by original sin, remains good enough to serve as the foundation for grace. Unlike the Reformers who tended to emphasise the sinfulness of human nature ('utter depravity' is the term used by Martin Luther), Catholicism holds a relatively sanguine view of the human person, one that is radically compatible with grace. This means that when grace interacts with human nature it does not have to destroy it in order to save it. Rather, grace *builds on* or *perfects* human nature. In a sense, we are made for grace; as human persons we are radically open to it.

grace perfects nature

To the extent that we find authentic, natural, human happiness, we are also open to supernatural happiness, for which we were ultimately created.

To the extent that we find authentic, natural, human happiness, we are also open to supernatural happiness, for which we were ultimately created. This is one of the most radical and distinctive features of Catholic theology. Unlike the Reformers who believed that human nature was too corrupted by sin to be dependable (a view that led many of them, especially Luther and Calvin, to reject natural law), Catholics believe that a great deal of knowledge about God's will can be derived from the use of reason alone.

To be sure, grace and revelation play an important part, but they do not change the material content of natural law. That is to say, both a non-believer and a Christian could arrive at exactly the same set of moral norms; they could both believe, for example, that murder, lying, theft, dishonouring one's parents and fornication were all immoral. The difference is that the Christian would have a clarified view of these norms and would also see that moral behaviour has an eschatological dimension to it. It is not just a question of natural human morality, but of our supernatural destiny. This eschatological view could provide the motivation even to give up one's life for another, a thought which might seem irrational to an unbeliever.

EXERCISE 6:

a) If most of our moral teaching is derived from natural law, what good is Scripture to us as we make moral choices? Write 10 lines.

[handwritten notes in top margin]

6. NATURAL LAW AND SPIRITUALITY

6.1 LIFE IN SOCIETY

The terms 'natural law' and 'spirituality' are seldom found in the same sentence. Spirituality tends to be seen as something personal, prayerful and Gospel-oriented, whereas natural law might be seen as philosophical and coldly rational. However, it should be apparent by now that Catholic morality is so deeply rooted in the natural law tradition that it would have to influence its understanding of spirituality as well. To begin with, the differences between morality and spirituality will be explored. Theologian, Michael Duffey of Marquette University, USA, defines spirituality as:

> The human movement toward the God revealed to Israel and through Jesus Christ that is manifested in greater wholeness of life through communion with others ... Recognition that Christian morality is a response to the divine grace and holiness offered to humankind through Jesus Christ suggests that morality and spirituality are being reunited. All of it recognises that the Christian moral quest to love neighbour is intimately related to our quest to know and love God.
>
> (Duffey, Michael: *Be Blessed in What You Do: The Unity of Christian Ethics and Spirituality*, 1988, New York, Paulist, p.32.)

Duffey emphasises that our movement towards God and Jesus occurs 'in greater wholeness of life through communion with others'. This clearly gives great importance to human wholeness and to life in society. He could even have said 'holiness and regular worship' but instead he began with the human reality and noted that we actually move towards God through them. It is also important to note that even though he was defining spirituality, we could substitute the word morality in the definition and it would still be accurate. So we see that morality and spirituality are closely related, perhaps even synonymous.

Morality and spirituality are closely related, perhaps even synonymous.

For Leonardo Boff, the liberation theologian, spirituality is even more concrete, even political. It involves:

a)   self discipline (asceticism) of solidarity with the needy;

b)   participation in community affairs;

c)   the ability to see the common good for future generations; and

d)   the advocating of appropriate action for the present.[4]

Again, we find here a clearly secular understanding of spirituality which could be embraced by any person of good will. Even accounting for the fact that Boff is biased toward a 'hands-on' type of spirituality that includes the transformation of social and political structures, his understanding here is clearly rooted in natural law.

These examples have not been mentioned in order to undermine or diminish the importance of Scripture, Christian discipleship or revelation. What is being shown is that a Catholic view of morality, rooted in natural law and reason, gives rise to a kind of spirituality that must pay attention to the real world and take its lessons seriously.

6.2 FEAR OF NATURE

Throughout history there have been repeated instances of heretical spiritualities which have denied the goodness of created reality. Manichaeism

---

4.   Boff, Leonardo: *Faith on the Edge: Religion and Marginalized Existence*, 1991, New York, Orbis; cited in Keating, James: 'Parishioners and Politics', *Church* (Fall 1992), p. 12.

Even some contemporary forms of Christian spirituality have fallen prey to an exaggerated asceticism based on a negative view of the human person.

in the fourth century and Albigensianism in the thirteenth century are but two examples. Both were gnostic heresies that had an extremely narrow understanding of what was spiritual. They fell outside of the Church's teaching because they refused to acknowledge the goodness and holiness of created things, especially those relating to sexuality. Even some contemporary forms of Christian spirituality have fallen prey to an exaggerated asceticism based on a negative view of the human person.

6.3   TRUST IN NATURE

Catholic spirituality, on the other hand, takes created reality seriously, even allowing earthly, created things such as water, oil, words and human commitments to become sacraments – mediations of God's grace. Even though Catholicism believes in the unique salvific role of Jesus Christ, it also believes that God's grace and invitation extend beyond the walls of the Church to non-believers. Just as they can achieve a good measure of moral goodness without the benefit of the Gospel, so they can, to some extent, hear and respond to God's call to salvation.

Natural law provides a sound approach to ethics and ecology. Careful observation of the environment leads us to see patterns and norms that contribute to the health of the planet. This is in part how the discipline of eco-spirituality evolved. It says that spirituality cannot be narrowly confined to individual persons or groups of persons without reference to their environment, but must also consider the whole eco-system of which we are a part.

EXERCISE 7:

a) *Describe the relationship between morality and spirituality? Write 5 lines.*

b) *Has spirituality ever influenced your moral decisions? Write 5 lines.*

c) *Have moral choices shaped your spirituality? Write 5 lines.*

SECTION THREE
THE MORAL DEVELOPMENT OF THE HUMAN PERSON

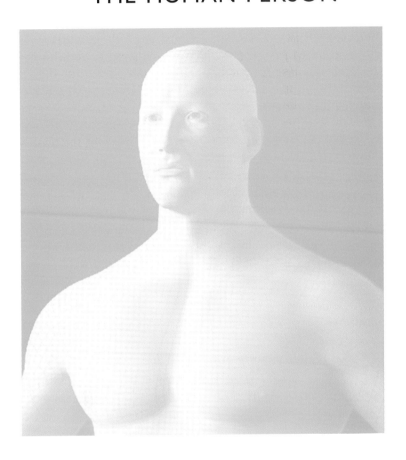

I.   TWO ACCOUNTS OF HUMAN DEVELOPMENT

In an earlier section entitled Morality and Law the distinction was raised
between autonomy and heteronomy to signify the difference between, on the
one hand, human acts that are based on a clear understanding and are
internally motivated, and on the other hand behaviour performed by persons
who lack full understanding of what they're doing and who feel somehow
constrained by laws. The argument at the end of this section will be that a
certain level of human development, based upon wise education, is
presupposed if a person is to achieve autonomy. This argument will entail
paying some attention to the ambiguity in the way the term *autonomy* is used in
our society, and refining our positive use of the term. The major part of what will
be done here, however, will be an attempt to grasp two important accounts of
human development and of moral consciousness in order to help us to read the
signs of an emerging autonomy in developmental terms.

2.   HUMANISATION

There is nothing new in the idea that there is a qualitative difference between
the moral sensibilities of different persons as a result of their varying growth

experiences and human maturation. One can point to the various ways in which the Greek philosophers Plato (427-347 bce) and Aristotle (384-322 bce) depicted the qualities of the person of virtue as an example. For instance, in his Nichomachaean Ethics, Aristotle insisted that the young should be able to learn moral behaviour by modelling themselves upon a person of virtue. In other words, by arriving at that balance and grace which are the fruit of virtue a person becomes an exemplar for others who are still undergoing this process of humanisation.

2.1   SØREN KIERKEGAARD

In the modern period, the idea that there exist patterns of development or stages of moral growth has come into its own. There are lots of examples, but two are especially well known. The nineteenth-century Danish philosopher Søren Kierkegaard (1813-1855 ce) developed a language for moral and theological development which has influenced theological reflection ever since. Kierkegaard spoke of three stages of human outlook which he imagined to be developmental. He called them the aesthetic, the moral and the religious stage.

- In the *aesthetic* stage, the person lives for pleasure and self-satisfaction – the aesthetic element being a reference here to the gratification of the sensory desires of the person.

- In Kierkegaard's *moral* stage, however, the individual becomes more conscious of his social context and begins to live with reference to the rights and interests of other persons. This so-called *moral* stage represents the product of a process of socialisation.

- Finally, in the *religious* stage, the person grasps that, as a creature, he or she exists to fulfill the good pleasure of the Creator, and as a Christian he or she lives to enable the solidarity of the body of Christ.

These classifications obviously draw upon Kierkegaard's own experience and upon his reading of Christian theology. Although he grounds himself in his own spiritual reflection rather than upon any empirical research, Kierkegaard's ideas remain noteworthy as an important early statement of a developmental scheme in theology.

2.2   WILLIAM JAMES

In the early twentieth century ce, the American psychologist William James (1842-1910 ce) described in his book The Varieties of Religious Experience the differences in moral and social sensibilities based in part upon temperament and genetic endowment, but based in part also upon character and experience. James devised the terms 'once-born' and 'twice-born' to characterise the difference between a kind of hard-boiled objectivity on the one hand, and a more sensitive symbolic empathy on the other hand. What is particularly interesting in James' account is his insight that experiences of apparent failure are very often responsible for helping us to redefine the sensibilities of the once-born so as to lead them into an appreciation (and even a participation) in the qualities of the twice-born.

William James was the brother of the influential writer Henry James. In the work of both brothers – William a psychologist and Henry a novelist – we find a highly-developed intuitive subjectivity that communicates deeply to readers and often persuades them to somehow change their lives.

2.3   SIGMUND FREUD

One more figure, much better known, who was surely responsible for shaping in a major way the research and writing on moral development in the twentieth century, was the founder of psychoanalysis, Sigmund Freud. At first, Freud contented himself with articulating the dynamics of the unconscious. But after considerable work with his patients, he began to realise that there is a developmental structure that begins in infancy (the oral, the anal and the genital periods) that represents human development in terms both of physical maturation and the symbolic focus of the unconscious mind. Although Freud developed his ideas of the moral person in the context of a therapeutic situation, his ideas became widely adopted in both scientific and literary circles. Certain Freudian terms and phrases have become part of the lexicon of educated people: unconscious, superego, libido, repression, etc.

3.   PIAGET AND KOHLBERG

This unit will now examine two psychologists whose work is empirically grounded, that is, those whose ideas are founded upon research with human subjects in a variety of different cultural contexts extended over many years. The theoretical categories of these psychologists – Jean Piaget and Lawrence Kohlberg – provide us with a framework for the analysis of moral thinking in terms of its developing capacities, and because these same ideas help us to grasp more clearly a positive understanding of autonomy and its importance for moral maturity.

The history of philosophy is to a great extent that of a certain clash of human temperaments ... I will write these traits down in two columns. I think you will practically recognise the two types of mental make-up that I mean if I head the columns by the titles 'tender-minded' and 'tough-minded' respectively.

THE TENDER-MINDED	THE TOUGH-MINDED
Rationalistic (going by 'principles')	Empiricist (going by 'facts')
Intellectualistic	Senstionalistic
Idealistic	Materialistic
Optimistic	Pessimistic
Religious	Irreligious
Free-willist	Fatalistic
Monistic	Pluralistic
Dogmatical	Sceptical

(William James, *Pragmatism: A New Way for Some Old Ways of Thinking*, 1907, New York, Longman Green, p.6)

EXERCISE 8:

Reflect on the ways in which you recognise different personality types in the people with whom you have contact. For example, some people are severe, and others are gentle; some are thoughtful, and others selfish. Make a list of some other contrasting distinctions of the same kind that you discover in your relationships with others.

a) Looking at your list of contrasting types, can you discover a relationship between the contrasts that you have made and the contrast between heteronomy and autonomy? Write 5 lines.

b) Have you yourself ever had a conversion of temperament of this kind, for example, moving from the controlling to the cooperative? Can you say why this change has occurred in you? Write 5 lines.

c) Can you grasp ways in which these differences of personality may play a role in moral judgment, the style of teaching, the quality of the human relationships or the spirit of a community? In a few lines, describe what you have learned in your reflection on this exercise.

4. JEAN PIAGET

Born in 1896 ce at Neuchâtel in Switzerland, Jean Piaget (1896-1980 ce) spent most of his life at the University of Geneva studying the evolving structures of logical thought. At one point, he imagined that he would be conducting what today we call 'life-span research', that is, a focus on the whole area of human development from birth to death. However, his discoveries concerning the development of structures of thinking in infants and children kept him focused for his whole lifetime upon the periods of mental development that lead up to the emergence of logical thinking in adolescence. In his long life as a research psychologist, Piaget contented himself with refining his accounts of these discoveries and solidifying the research upon which they were based.

4.1 GENETIC EPISTEMOLOGY

Piaget preferred to call his area of research 'genetic epistemology', two words which denote the unfolding of the structures of logical thinking. As Piaget put it:

> To explain intelligence genetically means to trace its development from the beginning and to show how it ends up in the final equilibrium of adolescent logical thinking. From this point of view, the work of psychology is comparable to work of embryology – work that is first of all descriptive and which consists in analysing the phases and the periods of the emergence of new forms, up to the ultimate stability constituted by adult morphology. This research can be called causal once the factors that assure movement from one stage to another have become evident.

(Piaget, Jean: *The Psychology of Intelligence*, 1947, English trans. 1950, New York, Harcourt Brace)

At one point in his training, Piaget underwent a training psychoanalysis (part of the formation for anyone preparing for a clinical role in medicine or psychology). Influenced in this way by the techniques of Sigmund Freud, Piaget developed his 'clinical method' for use in his own research. This was an interview method aimed to facilitate the free expression of his research subjects, rather than their focused response to a particular question.

For a few years as a young researcher Piaget had worked in Paris with Alfred Binet and his colleagues in their early research on IQ tests. In scoring the responses of children to these tests Piaget found himself especially fascinated by the wrong answers that children gave, and the fact that many different children seemed to give the same wrong answers to the questions posed by the IQ test. This led Piaget to wonder what kind of mental structure in these children might be responsible for these regularly given but obviously wrong answers. Convinced that he could discover how the children had constructed the meaning of the questions, he created research methods that facilitated the free expression of their ideas without scoring right or wrong answers. In his mind, the difference was not between right or wrong, but between one kind of thinking process and another.

What kind of mental structure in these children might be responsible for these regularly given but obviously wrong answers.

While still a young man, Piaget, on the basis of his early publications, was invited back to his native Switzerland to become director of research at the Jean-Jacques Rousseau Institute at the University of Geneva, where in fact he was destined to spend the rest of his professional life. Over a period of more than forty years, Piaget attempted to understand the evolution of logical thinking, beginning with the very earliest structures of thinking of the infant. In the paragraphs that follow, two aspects of Piaget's research will be examined:

- his account of the stages of development of human intelligence; and
- his account of the structures of moral thinking.

4.2   THE DEVELOPMENT OF HUMAN INTELLIGENCE

Piaget postulated four stages in the evolution of human thought toward logical adequacy. Here is a description of these stages:

Stage One: Sensorimotor Learning

In observing the behaviour of new-born infants, Piaget became impressed by the apparent hard work conducted by small infants, even in their earliest days. Watch a child during the first two months of life and you will see the repetition of the same movements over and over again – the opening and closing of the hands, the repeated movement of the muscles of the legs, head, mouth and jaw movements (quite apart from the sucking action used in nursing). Piaget called these 'circular movements', that is, repeated actions which allow the child to experience and finally to control the musculature of the body.

For Piaget, all of this was about learning. He called it sensorimotor learning, a phrase which means both learning how to use the body, and learning to build a foundation in the body for the more highly developed activities of speaking and conceptual thinking (a child is not able to speak until it has learned to control the muscles of the mouth, the jaw and the tongue). Another task for sensorimotor learning is the coordination of the eye and the hand. Little by little, usually with lots of encouragement from a parent, the infant begins to internalise the procedure of seeing something that it wants and discovering how to grasp it.

At the same time, the infant begins to distinguish between the action programs (Piaget calls them 'schemes') for sucking, for swallowing or for grasping. Gradually the infant identifies new means for achieving its fundamental ends, and this constitutes the beginning of *intention* – the interior movement of reflection and will that reaches out for an object using the chosen means.

intention

UNIT TWO
SECTION THREE

According to Piaget, the key moment in the positive development of sensorimotor thinking is the formation of the permanent object. Piaget's researches demonstrated a clear sequence in the development of the infant's capacity to understand an independent object outside itself. In summary, these were his findings:

a) at the earliest stage, an object which is hidden ceases to exist for the infant;

b) the beginning of a sense of permanence is tied to the child's activity: if a toy is hidden under one of two cushions and the child finds the toy under the one on the left, he will continue to look for the toy under the cushion on the left, even if the psychologist obviously hides it under the one on the right;

c) Somewhat later, the child will look immediately in the spot where it most recently *saw* the hidden object. Nonetheless, the child will not succeed if the search becomes complicated, requiring the inference of the presence of the toy in some place as yet unfamiliar;

d) only at the end of sensorimotor development (eighteen months to two years) will the child demonstrate a persistent capacity to search for a hidden object and to show that he knows that the existence of the object does not depend upon its being evident or not.

One implication of Piaget's studies is that the infant at the beginning is unable to distinguish between itself and its mother – there is a fusion of internal needs and maternal care.

One implication of Piaget's studies is that the infant at the beginning is unable to distinguish between itself and its mother – there is a fusion of internal needs and maternal care. Only after a certain number of 'failures' on the part of the mother to respond quickly enough to the infant's demands will the child gradually *construct* the idea that *milk-warmth-love* (the child's experience of 'mother') is something other than himself.

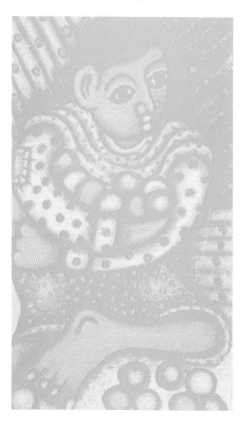

Piaget remarks that the successful evolution of sensorimotor thinking constitutes a kind of intellectual revolution for the child in the sense that the child de-centres his actions away from his own body and begins to appreciate that objects exist in space apart from himself and his own immediate desires. As the infant develops it achieves a gradual coordination of its actions, leading to the taken-for-granted relation between means and ends which characterises intelligence as such. The child thus takes the first steps away from the absolute dependency of its initial stages of infancy towards an interdependence with objects exterior to its own body.

Stage Two: Pre-Operational Thinking

The essential difference between the sensorimotor period and pre-operational behaviour is that in the first case the interactions of the child occur directly with its outside environment, whereas in the case of preoperations, the child begins to make use of symbols that represent this environment. The child begins to use words as signifiers for the objects around it. Progress is very slow, but nonetheless the child begins to recognise certain familiar patterns. At the end of the the sensorimotor period, the child recognises repeated sequences such as 'mother-with-coat-goes' and 'bowl-clink-eat' or 'pillow-thumb-sleep'. The child comes to anticipate the expected consequences of these actions. This is the beginning of the use of language, and it develops between the ages of two to five years.

The preoperational child, entering into the use of language, internalises these sequences and begins to use language to name what it knows. This linguistic capacity introduces the ability to reflect upon action. The process of language acquisition involves the assimilation of words understood within a personal system of meaning. Children hear and imitate other people, often without understanding what it is they are really saying. We are often amused when small children begin to speak using language far too sophisticated for their real understanding. Nonetheless, between two and four years of age, children build a vocabulary and enter into language understanding that allows them to participate in the social actions of the society around them.

Nonetheless, between two and four years of age, children build a vocabulary and enter into language understanding that allows them to participate in the social actions of the society around them.

The thinking of the preoperational child is mysterious. Children of this age love stories where fantastic solutions to difficult problems appear magically out of nowhere, offering them the imaginative compensation of achieving some great end without having to go through the hard (and sometimes impossible) work of figuring out how big people solve these problems in real life. The religious thinking of the preoperational child is likewise magical, and the prayers of these children regularly ask for and expect miracles (it is a shame, however, that frequently the religious thinking of adults remains fixated at this level).

Piaget's study of this period of a child's development is vast, and there is no way the richness of his research can be briefly summarised. It is clear that the introduction of language use changes the child's relationship to the world entirely. Just as learning to walk and then to run introduces the child, through mobility, to a new independence; so learning to use words represents a liberty of expression which obviously gives a great deal of pleasure to most children.

The introduction of language use changes entirely the child's relationship to the world.

This preoperational period is characterised by several qualities: concrete thinking, irreversible thinking, centred thinking and static thinking.

Concrete

To call the child's thinking here *concrete* means that it is tied directly to using words referring to very specific objects or actions. The child at this point does not have a variety of experiences to nuance its understanding; it is unable to analyse or synthesise its experience. There is as yet no process of reflection. The child's thinking is immediate and non-contextualised: it is only about the here-and-now.

Irreversible

Irreversible thinking means the incapacity to recognise the implications of relationships between objects as they are in themselves. It is not surprising that the child at the preoperational stage is unable to reason out what seems obvious to an adult. Here is an interesting example of preoperational thinking. Piaget posed this question to a child of four years:

> 'Do you have a brother?' The response, 'Yes'.
> 'What's his name?' The response, 'Jimmy'.
> 'And does Jimmy have a brother?' The response, 'No, he doesn't'.

In this child's mind, the relation is irreversible – it is all seen from the point of view of the child himself.

Egocentric

Piaget also calls the thinking of this stage *egocentric* or *centred*, in the sense that the child is unable to take the point of view of another person. He may use words which have meaning only for himself, and then be surprised if you don't understand. This kind of thinking frequently pays attention to only one detail of an object, but neglects other aspects.

Static

Finally preoperational thought is *static*. At this stage the child cannot conceive of the transformation whereby an object changes its state or condition. Pouring the same liquid from a wide squat vessel into a narrow tall vessel, the child will judge that there is more liquid in the second vessel because the level is visually higher than in the former one. Ask a child to draw the intermediate positions of a rod that falls from vertical to horizontal position, and he will not be able to imagine and symbolise in drawings the gradual transformation. He or she will not as yet know how to do so.

Before moving on, a word must be said about the terminology being used here. For Piaget, 'operation' is a word that means 'logic' or a mental action that works on the environment. Therefore, preoperational means pre-logical, even though we can see in this period the slow emergence of the structures that become the foundation for logical operations: language use, enriched experience and a growing repertory of symbolic expressions for that experience.

Stage Three: Interaction

Concrete operational thinking begins at the age of five or six only when the child has learned to coordinate the physical operations of his body and has entered the world of language. At about the age of five and a half, the child begins to understand more clearly the social world. Piaget observed that while children who were preoperational enjoyed the company of other children and adults, they did not begin to really interact meaningfully with others before operational thinking had developed. It is only at this point that real social exchanges begin for the first time.

At this age children are introduced to the schoolroom. This is the level at which they begin to learn all the lore of their culture. The operational child typically enjoys learning and takes pride in being able to explain things to others. The child begins to have logical insight into directly observed, concrete reality. He learns reversibility in mathematical problems, recognising at last that if $3 + 5 = 8$, then also $8 - 5 = 3$; or, in a language problem, if all men and all women equal all the adults of the world; then all the adults minus all the men equals all the women. The ability to process complex (but concrete) relationships becomes easier and makes sense.

Thanks to logical reversibility, the child begins to *de-centre* his thinking away from his own personal perspective and to enter into relations of reciprocity, thus beginning to take on another person's point of view. This change in relationship affects the structures of his thinking. Physical growth, the enlargement of his circle of relationships and a growing list of new learning experiences – particularly those structured systematically by the curriculum of the school – lead the child gradually to the threshold of formal logic.

It is noteworthy that in some pedagogical systems, such as Montessori or Steiner schools, operational thinking is taught in such a way as to incorporate sensorimotor activity. The learning materials of the Montessori school provide the child with rods or beads to manipulate as he or she learns introductory arithmetic. Letters made of sandpaper provide a sensorimotor accompaniment which allow the child to associate the shape of the letter with the symbol it represents. And wherever possible, some sensory learning aide is devised to help the child understand and internalise what must be learned. In this way, action in the mind is always accompanied by action in the world of sense experience.

During this operational period, the fundamental learning skills of the child – reading, spelling, writing and arithmetic – are acquired. Although children can become excited at this level by their interest in what they learn, it still remains fundamentally a period of mental accommodation, in comparison with the final stage which follows it.

Stage Four: Deductive and Creative Logic

Formal operational thinking and the development of the structures for deductive and creative logic begin at about the age of twelve. If concrete operations led the growing child to a capacity for deductive logic, then formal operations open up a new period which leads thought beyond the immediate and concrete and into the world of the possible. With concrete operations, the child was always linked directly to an experience, and the child extrapolated data from the testimony of its senses. In adolescence, formal operations introduce a kind of thinking which focuses upon possibilities, hypotheses, and what we might refer to as 'what if?' thinking. At this stage, the adolescent begins to imagine a world without limits, seeking always to introduce alternatives and the experimental. This explains teenagers' passion for movies such as *Star Wars*, electronic games, and gadgets of every kind.

Within the realm of education, formal operational thinking is used to solve complicated mathematical equations including not only reversibility, but also the combining of multiple systems of relationships – problems that involve not only mathematical reasoning, but thought experiments as well.

From the point of view of Piaget's epistemology, formal thinking is the fruit of a continual process of adaptation, balancing two dynamics that are constantly in interaction:

- *assimilation*: this is the process of incorporating elements from the environment into the structure of thinking, often creating internal challenges as a result of experiencing new data and new methods of attack; and

- *accommodation*: this is the process by which thinking modifies its structures or schemes so as to be able to understand and treat new experiences adequately.

The interaction of these two dynamics of adaptation is called *equilibration*, meaning the movement towards balance or equilibrium of a dynamic cognitive organism always in the process of experiencing new challenges.

Physical growth, the enlargement of his circle of relationships and a growing list of new learning experiences – particularly as these are structured systematically by the curriculum of the school – lead the child gradually to the threshold of formal logic.

in some pedagogical systems, such as Montessori or Steiner schools, operational thinking is taught in such a way as to incorporate sensorimotor activity.

UNIT TWO
SECTION THREE

assimilation

accommodation

equilibration

constructivism

In a similar way, Piaget refers to another characteristic of human thinking which he calls *constructivism*. By this term, he means that the subject is always in the process of constructing, either by way of language or new forms of intelligence, a renewed account of how he or she understands the world. For our purposes here, given the strong social bias of Piaget's thinking, it might be better to refer to this dynamic as *co-construction* because at the operational and formal levels, thinking is always conceived in a context of relationships (something that is explained elsewhere in this module).

It is possible, then, to understand how Piaget's research explains why the early formal thinking of the adolescent is characterised by creativity and passion.

It is possible, then, to understand how Piaget's research explains why the early formal thinking of the adolescent is characterised by creativity and passion. The young person entering for the first time into hypothetical thinking finds pleasure in imagining a different and ideal world. One can see here the awakening of the utopian instinct.

EXERCISE 9:

Piaget referred to the 'construction' of ways of thinking, a phrase which highlights the active role of the moral subject and also the constant fine-tuning of the thinking process itself. Piaget wanted to get away from a structure that was so rigid that it could only conceive of one right answer for any essential question. Beginning with the moral experience of the child, he wanted to demonstrate that real questions are couched in lived situations, and real responses involve a creative and active engagement of the moral subject (who has learned, of course, important things about his or her tradition).

a) Describe how you yourself sometimes get stuck in your thinking processes. Describe how a 'constructive' model of unthinking has potential to liberate people from dead-ends. Write 10 lines.

b) Can you think of a poem, a story, or a Gospel passage that illustrates the appeal to open-ended thinking? Write 5 lines.

4.3 PIAGET'S ANALYSIS OF MORAL THINKING

In 1932 ce Piaget published a book which unleashed a wave of research which has had a great impact on educational theory and religious education. Using the structures of genetic epistemology, he addressed in his book *The Moral Judgment of the Child* the question of how moral thinking develops.

It was from Kant that Piaget took the terms we introduced already in the last chapter, heteronomy and autonomy.

In all his work, Piaget consistently showed the relationship between his research findings and the doctrines and categories of the great philosophers. So, in a very natural way, Piaget borrowed from the German philosopher Kant the categories that he felt would best explain what he discovered. It was from Kant that he took the terms we introduced already in the last chapter, *heteronomy* and *autonomy*.

For Piaget all morality consists in a system of rules.

Although the earlier section on morality and law takes a perspective which differs from that of Piaget, it should be noted that for Piaget all morality consists in a system of rules, and therefore for him the essence of all morality is to understand the quality of respect which the individual accords to these rules. Small children accept from adults fully elaborated rules handed down over a span of generations. In order to enter the perspective of the child, Piaget sought for some structure or social experience governed by rules which was natural to the life of small children. He landed upon the game of marbles, which in Switzerland (surprise to say) in the 1930's had a fully codified structure.

With respect to the rules of the game, Piaget identified four successive stages in the child's comprehension of rules:

a)   a purely motor and individual stage in which the child handles the marbles at whim without any awareness of collective rules;

b)   an egocentric stage (aged two to five) when the child notices the example of rules used by other children, but continues to play either by himself (without finding playmates) or with others (without trying to win). At this stage, everyone can win at once, since nobody really understands the rules;

c)   the stage of initial cooperation (between seven and eight) when each player tries to win. While agreement may be reached for the course of one game, children of this age who play together nonetheless give contradictory accounts of the rules observed; and

d)   finally, around the age of eleven or twelve, there begins the stage of codification of rules. Every detail in the game is fixed, and the code of rules is known fully to everyone involved.

Heteronomy

What is more important than this evolution according to age and development of thinking, however, is the progression in the meaning of rules across these stages. During the first motor/individual stage, rules are not yet coercive in character, because they are received unconsciously as examples of the behaviour of others, but are not yet obligatory. In the second and the third stages – those of the egocentric and initial cooperation stages – rules are regarded as sacred and untouchable, handed down by adults and therefore unchangeable. Any alteration in the rules strikes the child as a transgression. Finally, around the age of twelve, a rule is looked upon as a law based on mutual consent, which one must respect on the basis of one's relationship with one's partners. However, the alteration of rules is permissible on the condition of common agreement within the group.

Around the age of twelve, a rule is looked upon as a law based on mutual consent, which one must respect on the basis of one's relationship with one's partners.

Piaget considered the first three examples as expressions of *heteronomy*, involving obedience without full understanding of norms; this happens at first without internalisation, but then later it is rigidly internalised. Rules at this stage constitute a kind of threat, and breaking the rules leads to punishment or disapproval. Submitting to the rules is the price one pays for participating in social experiences.

Submitting to the rules is the price one pays for participating in social experiences.

Autonomy

The fourth stage, however, represents for Piaget what he calls *autonomy*. Piaget says:

> Co-operation alone leads to autonomy. With regard to logic, co-operation is at first a source of criticism; thanks to the mutual control which it introduces, it suppresses both the spontaneous conviction that characterises egocentrism and the blind faith in adult authority … It is … absurd and even immoral to wish to impose upon the child a fully worked-out system of discipline when the social life of children among themselves is sufficiently developed to give rise to a discipline indefinitely nearer to that inner submission which is the mark of adult morality.

(Piaget, Jean: *The Moral Judgment of the Child*, (trans. 1932). New York, Harcourt, Brace Jovanovich, pp.403-4)

Co-operation and Social Restraint

There is one final point in Piaget's research that requires our attention here. Piaget discovered that the relation of the subject to the rule (or law) corresponds to the form of relation between the subject and other people. Inner responsibility or *autonomy* arises from relations of *cooperation*. An autonomous moral attitude replaces a heteronomous one as a result of the moral climate of the relationship.

A climate of social constrain results in a form of authority analogous to that exercised by adult constraint on the mind of the small child.

In a parallel fashion, *social constraint*, in which there is an element of non-dialogical authority and which is not the result of an interchange between individuals who relate as peers, generates a climate of *heteronomy*. Such a climate results in a form of authority analogous to that exercised by adult constraint on the mind of the small child.

Every exercise of authority profits from consultation, dialogue and open and mutual understanding.

Every exercise of authority profits from consultation, dialogue and open and mutual understanding. Such procedures do not constitute an abandonment of authority. Quite the contrary, they represent the use of authority in such a way as to maximise its influence and to promote the autonomy, internalisation and willing cooperation of the members of the group (see Piaget, Jean: The Moral Judgment of the Child (trans. 1932), New York, Harcourt, Brace Jovanovich, pp.339-340).

Effective leaders listen carefully to their subordinates and generate credibility for their authority by their approachability and their attention to the perspectives and concerns of those who work with and for them. This is as true in working with adults as with children.

4.4   SUMMARY

What has been conveyed in this brief sampling of Piaget's research is the relation between understanding and responsibility.

What has been conveyed in this brief sampling of Piaget's research is the relation between understanding and responsibility. The moral thinking of the human person, like logical thinking, is always in a state of evolution (*equilibration*) if it is alive and healthy. The healthy person is constantly engaged in co-constructing and re-balancing (*equilibrating*) his or her moral understanding.

Autonomy for Piaget required an ongoing dialogue with one's peers as the context for receiving the moral tradition of society. Piaget denied neither tradition nor authority, but rather he insisted that adult forms of logic and of moral thinking require the internalisation of the rules and the creative application of the tradition to actual circumstances. Occasionally parents wonder why they have so little success in transmitting their norms or ideas to a new generation. Certainly one part of the answer has to do with how little adults seem to understand the essential role of promoting *autonomy* in leading others to new ideas and traditional values of their own.

There exists in the child certain attitudes and beliefs which intellectual development will more and more tend to eliminate.

There is an adult in every child and a child in every adult. The difference in nature reduces itself to this. There exists in the child certain attitudes and beliefs which intellectual development will more and more tend to eliminate: there are others which will acquire more and more importance. The latter are not simply derived from the former but are partly antagonistic to them. The two sets of phenomena are to be met both in the child and in the adult, but one set predominates in the one, the other in the other …

There are therefore no inclusive stages which define the whole of a subject's mental life at a given point of his evolution; the stages should be thought of as successive phases of regular processes recurring like a rhythm on the superposed planes of behaviour and consciousness. A given individual may, for example, have reached the stage of autonomy with regard to a certain group of rules, while his consciousness of these rules, together with the practice of certain more subtle rules, will still be coloured with heteronomy. We cannot therefore speak of global or inclusive stages characterised as such by autonomy or heteronomy, but only of phases of heteronomy or autonomy which define a process that is repeated for each new set of rules or for each new plane of reflection.

(Piaget, Jean: The Moral Judgment of the Child, pp.85-86)

5. THE MORAL SYSTEM OF LAWRENCE KOHLBERG

5.1 A LIFE-SPAN FRAMEWORK

 In 1958, the American psychologist Lawrence Kohlberg (1927-1987 ce) published a doctoral thesis from the University of Chicago which had as its goal the describing of the dynamics of moral development after the pattern of Piaget, but beyond the age of adolescence. Kohlberg replaced Piaget's two moral categories of heteronomy and autonomy with his own system structured in terms of three levels and six stages. He based his research on the same type of clinical interviews that Piaget had used. However, Kohlberg remarked that as soon as he began his research with children, he saw that there were a variety of ways in which norms that had not been interiorised were expressed – often in a confused fashion that had nothing to do with the influence of parents, teachers or even peers. He felt that he needed a broader vocabulary to express this variety and to describe the changing relation of the moral subject to the social order.

Kohlberg's description of his six stages will be provided below so that the overall shape of his program can be seen. However, what is of most interest here is his idea of the three levels that represent the relationship of the moral individual to the expectations of society. He describes these three levels with reference to a term which is not overly familiar in daily conversation – 'convention'. A convention refers to a practice or procedure widely observed in a social group – it means the same thing as a custom. When used as an adjective, the word 'conventional' means something based on, or in accordance with, general use or practice – that which is customary.

Kohlberg sets up the framework for his appreciation of moral development by claiming that each person has a developmental trajectory (a gamut of predictable transformations) that runs from the pre-conventional, through the conventional and (in many cases) into the post-conventional. It will be important to examine his understanding of these categories. For analysing moral reactions and moral behaviour, these three categories can prove very useful for a moral theologian.

Kohlberg felt that he needed a broader vocabulary to express this variety and to describe the changing relation of the moral subject to the social order.

convention

5.2 MORAL THINKING AT THE PRE-CONVENTIONAL LEVEL

First, let's look at Kohlberg's description of this level:

> At this level, the child is responsive to cultural rules and labels of good and bad, right or wrong, but interprets these labels in terms of either the physical or the hedonistic consequences of action (punishment, reward, exchange of favours) or in terms of the physical power of those who enunciate the rules and labels.

(Kohlberg, Lawrence: *Essays on Moral Development*, vol. 1, 1981, Harper & Row, San Francisco, p.17)

In general, the preconventional moral level evokes an ethos of pressure and discomfort. The moral subject is never completely clear what must be done, or exactly why it must be done in a certain way. This level is often characterised by misunderstandings of what ought to be done. As a result, there is a lack of freedom and a lack of full investment on the part of the moral subject.

We should remember Piaget's advice about the character of autonomy or heteronomy in different domains of human experience. Quite often, someone who is autonomous in some areas (particularly where he or she has certain

It is frequently the case that the state of heteronomy lingers most decidedly in the areas of morality and religion.

responsibilities, such as at work) will be heteronomous in others. It is frequently the case that the state of heteronomy lingers most decidedly in the areas of morality and religion. That may be because we receive our moral and religious ideas from others for a very long time – others who insist on exact norms from their position as authoritative representatives of a tradition. Often enough, a person's spontaneous response to a question of moral decision-making will be, 'Oh, that's too complicated!' Such a reaction is a regression into pre-conventional heteronomy.

Asking children or even adults to reason about their moral decision-making is certainly a good way to invite them to enhance the autonomous quality of their moral thinking. But most often, those who are operating at a pre-conventional level have no great interest in looking critically at such questions. They prefer to dismiss such discussion as something about which they have almost no interest.

5.3   MORAL THINKING AT THE CONVENTIONAL LEVEL

Kohlberg's explanation of the conventional is as follows:

> At this level, maintaining the expectations of the individual's family, group, or nation is perceived as valuable in its own right, regardless of immediate and obvious consequences. The attitude is not only one of conformity to personal expectations and social order, but of loyalty to it, of actively maintaining, supporting, and justifying the order and of identifying with the people or group involved in it.
>
> (Kohlberg, Lawrence: *Essays on Moral Development*, vol. 1, 1981, Harper & Row, San Francisco, p.18)

At this level of conventional thinking, the person (the moral subject) identifies with what we might call the 'standard account' of social explanations. He or she buys into the official position of the organisation, the state or the nation. In this way, the conventional moral agent becomes a supporter and a sponsor of the tradition and of those who hold positions of authority. From a detached point of view, we might say that conventional reasoning possesses an 'excess of clarity' in the sense that such persons fail to appreciate the complexity of difficult cases or possible alternatives to the status quo.

There is clearly a kind of autonomy of cooperation at this level, since the moral agent is intentionally cooperating with others towards a goal that stimulates passionate investment. It is sobering to remember, however, that people who have been conventional thinkers in a fascist state like Nazi Germany felt good about being contributing members of what they considered an authoritative social order. At the conventional level, tradition and its laws are believed to solve all problems. The social order becomes, as it were, frozen – unable to move beyond what is fixed in the prescriptions of the law. As a result, people can become stuck in an official system which manipulates public opinion and fails to invite them to a critical reflection on difficult issues. This is why the next level is so important.

5.4   THE POSTCONVENTIONAL OR AUTONOMOUS LEVEL

Kohlberg defines this level as follows:

> There is a clear effort to define moral values and principles that have validity and application apart from the authority of the groups or people holding these principles, and apart from the individual's own identification with these groups.

(Kohlberg, Lawrence: *Essays on Moral Development*, vol. 1, 1981, Harper & Row, San Francisco, p.18)

This postconventional level represents a kind of conscientious objection to the lack of flexibility in the legal system or its laws. An example which Kohlberg often used to illustrate a postconventional choice is the conscientious objection of someone conscripted by the law into military service (a burning question in the United States at the time Kohlberg conceived his research). He drew other examples from the resistance of citizens to the official authority of leaders in a fascist regime, Nazi Germany being the best-known example.

A postconventional ethos or attitude is usually arrived at as the result of a painful process of reflection and discernment. Because the levels and stages of moral development as conceived by Kohlberg are both developmental (gradually emerging) and hierarchical (the later stages building upon and presuming the earlier ones), the postconventional person can be neither an untutored narcissist nor an antisocial anarchist. Rather, the postconventional ethos appreciates the positive aspects of social construction (all that has been contributed by the first two levels). But this person also recognises the incapacity of the conventional order to respond to delicate problems of some groups and persons in the broader society.

The postconventional person can be neither an untutored narcissist nor an antisocial anarchist.

In both Europe and America at present there are huge debates raging about immigration of peoples from Africa and Asia into Europe and from the Latin countries of Central and South America into the United States. This is a complicated matter, but nonetheless it seems clear that the debate pits conventional concerns about law and order (which would exclude immigrants who have entered the country illegally) against postconventional compassion for those who, although illegal entrants, have begun to settle, make social contributions and who additionally have genuine need for political sanctuary or social acceptance.

It goes without saying that the postconventional ethos is conscious of ambiguity. Indeed, it is always aware of the inescapable note of ambiguity that necessarily accompanies a conflict between law and order, on the one hand, and a search for a reasonable or compassionate response to a conflicted situation, on the other hand. It is fair to describe Kohlberg's idea of the postconventional as a creative freedom – a search for alternatives in the face of some legalistic dead ends. This is why the postconventional can be considered an example of prophetic daring.

The postconventional can be considered an example of prophetic daring.

Think of the non-violent protests led by Martin Luther King, for example, in the U.S. in the 1960s, or of the large demonstrations and social actions held throughout Europe against the Iraq war. King and his companions accepted the vulnerability of their position by placing themselves in opposition to unjust laws for the sake of calling attention to the moral and social evil caused by them. King was jailed several times for breaking the law. Such a person desires not to destroy the social tradition, but to renew it.

Kohlberg's description of his Stage Six evokes the content of this postconventional spirit:

> Right is defined by the decision of conscience in accord with self-chosen ethical principles appealing to logical comprehensiveness, universality, and consistency. These principles are abstract (the Golden Rule, the categorical imperative); they are not concrete moral rules such as the Ten Commandments.
>
> (Kohlberg, Lawrence: *Essays on Moral Development*, vol. 1, 1981, Harper & Row, San Francisco, p. 19)

5.5   SIX STAGES OF MORAL DEVELOPMENT

A Characterisation of the Six Stages of Moral Development, by Lawrence Kohlberg

Preconventional Level

Stage 1. Obey rules to avoid punishment (the value of human life is confused with the value of physical objects and is based on the social status or physical attributes of the possessor).

Stage 2. Conform to obtain rewards, have favours returned, and so on (the value of human life is seen as instrumental to the satisfaction of the needs of its possessor or of other people).

Conventional Level

Stage 3. Conform to avoid disapproval and dislike by others (the value of human life is based on the empathy and affection of family members and others toward its possessor).

Stage 4. Conform to avoid censure by legitimate authorities and resultant guilt (life is conceived as sacred in terms of its place in a categorical moral or religious order of rights and duties).

Postconventional Level

Stage 5. Conform to maintain the respect of the impartial spectator judging in terms of community welfare (life is valued both in terms of its relation to community welfare and in terms of life being a universal human right).

Stage 6. Conform to avoid self-condemnation (human life is sacred—a universal human value of respect for the individual).

(Kohlberg, Lawrence: *Essays on Moral Development*, 1981, San Francisco, Harper & Row, pp.19-29)

6.   THE STRUCTURES OF MORAL DEVELOPMENT

6.1   OVERCOMING AMBIGUITY

Clearly the term *autonomy* is ambiguous in our culture. For a long time, the word autonomy elicited a reaction of shocked disapproval from authority figures (especially in the Church). The Second Vatican Council, however, employed the term in the sense in which we have been using it here to mean a laudable independence of spirit and a creativity of imagination in addressing one's responsibilities.[5]

---

5.   See, for example, *Pastoral Constitution on the Church in the Modern World*, #55, 59, 71, 75, 77.

We should always remain aware of what we have learned about autonomy from its genesis in human development. Autonomy has a highly-complicated structure of evolution. It arises in the education and nurture provided by a family and community that supply essential confidence to the person; it emerges clearly in the context of cooperation; and it has an inescapable concern for the well-being of the community and for the common good.

We have all heard the term *autonomy* misused in ways that suggest an antisocial or selfish inclination on the part of an individual. But that is a misuse of the term. We must also be careful to distinguish between any form of selfishness (in the face of the conflict of interest between spouses, partners or friends) and *autonomy*. As Kohlberg's postconventional profile demonstrates, genuine *autonomy* is willing to suffer for the common good.

Autonomy implies a constant search to understand more profoundly. It is interesting to note that Piaget decided that one of the ways to judge the capacity for autonomous thinking is the ability of the moral subject to paraphrase what he or she has learned – to put it in their own words. This is also a good method for deepening one's understanding in any learning process. In pastoral care, it is very helpful when the pastoral minister is able to quietly paraphrase what he or she is hearing in an interview, both to make sure that they are getting the details correctly, but also to invite a further clarification on the part of the person in need.

6.2   FACING UP TO INJUSTICE

THE SCALES OF INJUSTICE

In any developed society, people will feel a very strong inclination to remain in the comfort zone of 'what everybody thinks and does'. We all feel the comforting tug of the conventional centre. Kohlberg's way of phrasing the challenges of moral development show us, however, that a full autonomy is a weighing of values that listens carefully to the demands of conscience, while simultaneously accepting the risks of speaking up in the face of injustices hidden by the authorities.

6.3   BROADER UNDERSTANDING

Even though creative responses can be unpredictable (and therefore more difficult to deal with), educators will always aim at the full moral education of all. The scope of moral growth should be as widely understood as possible –

even to the region of postconventional thinking and behaviour. This type of thinking is clear enough in the teaching of the Second Vatican Council and in most good contemporary theology. But, as we have just noted, we must also repeat that postconventional thinking can never be narcissistic or selfish. In actual experience, it will always require a delicate balance between individual conscience and the legal authority, between personal interest and the common good.

EXERCISE 10:

Piaget noted that there is frequently a failure of integration among the different realms of experience in which people live. Someone who is autonomous in their professional life may well remains heteronomous in his or her moral or religious thinking and behaviour. Use the terms of both Piaget and Kohlberg to explore the meaning of these ideas in your own experience:

a) Do you find yourself on the defensive in certain areas of your life? Where is it that you don't know enough, or fail to be free enough, to really express your deepest self? Write 5 lines.

b) What is the relation between study and moral freedom? Put another way, practically speaking, what does adequate 'conscience formation' mean to you now? Can you express this in terms of autonomy and in terms of the levels of Kohlberg's system? Write 5 lines.

c) How is moral freedom related to age, experience and development? Where do you see the challenges for the adult moral formation of people in your parish or your community? Write 5 lines.

CONCLUSIONS TO UNIT TWO

I.   LAW, GRACE AND NATURE

In setting out to study moral theology through an analysis of several key words – nature and law, reason and growth – a fifth word, 'grace', continually turns up. The precise relationship which grace has to each of the other concepts has been very controversial throughout the history of Christianity. What this unit has attempted to do is to set out the basic meaning of several key concepts which will be used over and over again in the study of individual moral issues. Even the few fundamental concepts which have been examined – for example, law – can be shown to have different meanings when used in different contexts. A non-believer will not accept some uses of the term law which a believer accepts, neither will the concept of nature be quite the same when used by a believer and a non-believer.

The one area where both believer and non-believer meet is in the area of human reason. Since a great deal of Christian morality, especially Catholic morality, is based on natural law, it requires the use of reason to decipher. At this level, the believer and the non-believer can dialogue with ease, using the same categories of goodness and the common good as a background against which moral arguments can proceed. This shared territory allows the Church great accessibility to public debates on moral issues of world importance.

2.   LEARNING OUTCOMES ASSESSED

Having completed this unit, the student should:

a)   be able to demonstrate how different moral theologies place differing importance on autonomy and theonomy;

b)   be competent in applying the principles of moral theology to particular cases, and even be able to do so using different moral theories;

c) respect the role and importance which the Catholic moral tradition gives to natural law, and hence to reason;

d) be clear about how natural law and reason relate to revelation in any debate on a moral issue; and

e) have a clear idea that modern research by some psychologists both accepts and endorses the Christian moral tradition.

BIBLIOGRAPHY

Aquinas, Thomas: *Commentary on the Sentences of Peter Lombard*.

— *Disputatio De Malo*, II.

— *Expositio de Trinitate*, II, 3.

— *Summa Theologiae*.

Aristotle: *Nicomachean Ethics*.

— *The Politics*.

Atkins, E.M. and Williams, Thomas (eds.): *Aquinas: Disputed Questions on the Virtues*, 2005, Cambridge, Cambridge University Press.

Augustine, *De Civitate Dei*.

— *De Libero Arbitrio*.

— *City of God*, (trans. by Walsh, G. et al.), 1958, Garden City, Image Books.

Auxerre, William of: *Summa Aurea*, translation in Crowe, *The Changing Profile of the Natural Law*, 1977, The Hague, Nijhoff.

Ayer, A.J.: *Language, Truth and Logic*, 1952, New York, Dover Publications.

Beauchamp, T., and Childress, James F.: *Principles of Biomedical Ethics*, 1983 (1989, 1994), New York/Oxford, Oxford University Press.

Bentham, Jeremy: *Introduction to the Principles of Morals and Legislation* (reprinted from the 1823 edition), 1948, New York, Hafner Publication Company.

Bilgrien, Marie Vianney: 'The Voices of Women in Moral Theology', in *America*, 173, no.20, p.14.

Boff, Leonardo: *Faith on the Edge: Religion and Marginalized Existence*, 1991, New York, Orbis.

Bouchard, Charles: 'Recovering the Gifts of the Holy Spirit in Moral Theology', in *Theological Studies*, September (62) 2002, pp.539-558.

Boyle, Leonard: *The Setting of the Summa Theologiae of Saint Thomas*, 1982, Toronto, Pontifical Institute of Medieval Studies.

Catechism of the Catholic Church.

Cicero: *Rhetoric*.

Crowe, Michael: *The Changing Profile of the Natural Law*, 1977, The Hague, Nijhoff.

Damascene, John: *De Fide Orthodoxa*. 1.2, Ch.22; MG 94945.

Davies, Brian: *The Thought of Thomas Aquinas*, 1992, Oxford, Clarendon Press.

Duffey, Michael: *Be Blessed in What You Do: The Unity of Christian Ethics and Spirituality*, 1988, New York, Paulist.

Fagan, Sean: *Does Morality Change?*, 2003, Dublin, The Columba Press.

Gilby, Thomas (ed.): *St Thomas Aquinas: Theological Texts*, 1982, Durham, North Carolina, Labyrinth Press.

Goodpaster, Kenneth: *Conscience and Corporate Culture*, 2006, Oxford, Blackwell.

Gula, Richard: *Reason Informed by Faith*, 1989, New York, Paulist Press.

Hannon, Patrick (ed.): Moral Theology – a Reader, 2006, Dublin, Veritas.

Hauerwas, Stanley: *A Community of Character*, 1981, Notre Dame, University of Notre Dame Press.

John Paul II: 1981, *Laborem Exercens*.

Keane, Philip: *Christian Ethics and Imagination: A Theological Inquiry*, 1984, New York, Paulist Press.

Keating, James: 'Parishioners and Politics', in *Church* (Fall 1992), p. 12.

Kennedy T.: *Doers of the Word: Moral Theology for the Third Millennium*, vol. I, 1996, Liguori Publications.

Kohlberg, Lawrence: *Essays on Moral Development*, vol. 1, 1981, Harper & Row, San Francisco.

Mahoney, John: 'The Classical Theory of the Moral Judgment', in *Seeking the Spirit: Essays in Moral and Pastoral Theology*, 1981, London and Denville, New Jersey, Sheed and Ward and Dimension Books, pp.52-62.

—   *The Making of Moral Theology: A Study of the Roman Catholic Tradition*, 1987, New York, Oxford.

Maritain, Jacques: 'On Knowledge through Connaturality', in *Range of Reason*, 1952, New York, Scribner, pp.26-7.

McCabe, Herbert: *Aquinas on Good Sense*, New Blackfriars, Vol. 67, pp. 419-431.

McDermott, T., (trans. and ed.): *Summa Theologiae — A Concise Translation*, 1989, Allen Texas, Christian Classics.

McDonagh, Enda: *The Making of Disciples*, 1982, Wilmington, Delaware, Glazier.

Moore, G.E.: *Principia Ethica*, reprinted 1968, Cambridge, CUP.

Nelson, Daniel Mark: *The Priority of Prudence: Virtue and Natural Law in Thomas Aquinas and the Implications for Modern Ethics*, 1992, Pennsylvania, University of Pennsylvania Press.

Nelson's Complete Concordance to the New American Bible, 1977, Nashville, Nelson.

Piaget, Jean: *The Moral Judgment of the Child*, (trans. 1932). New York, Harcourt, Brace Jovanovich.

Pinckaers, Servais: 'Virtue is Not A Habit', in *CrossCurrents* (Winter 1962), pp.65-88.

Plato: The Republic.

Regan, Richard J: *Aquinas: The Cardinal Virtues*, 2005, Indianapolis, Hackett Publishing Co.

Sparks, Richard C.: 'The Storm Over Proportionalism', in *Church* (Spring 1989), pp. 9-14.

Spohn, William: *What Are They Saying About Scripture and Ethics?*, revised edition, 1995, New York, Paulist.

Stump, Eleonore: *Aquinas*, 2003, London, Routledge.

The Catholic Study Bible, 1990, New York/Oxford, University Press.

Vacek, Edward: 'Proportionalism, One View of the Debate', in *Theological Studies* 46 (1985), pp.287-314.

Vatican II: *The Church in the Modern World*.

Walsh, Liam: *Theology for Today: Introduction to Theology*, 2005, Tallaght, The Priory Institute,

FURTHER READING

Davies, Brian: *The Thought of Thomas Aquinas*, 1992, Oxford, Clarendon Press.

Fagan, Sean: *Does Morality Change?*, 2003, Dublin, The Columba Press.

Goodpaster, Kenneth: *Conscience and Corporate Culture*, 2006, Oxford, Blackwell.

Hannon, Patrick (ed.): Moral Theology – a Reader, 2006, Dublin, Veritas.

Kennedy T.: *Doers of the Word: Moral Theology for the Third Millennium*, vol. I, 1996, Liguori Publications.

Mahoney, John: *The Making of Moral Theology: A Study of the Roman Catholic Tradition*, 1987, New York, Oxford.

McDermott, T., (trans. and ed.): *Summa Theologiae – A Concise Translation*, 1989, Allen Texas, Christian Classics.

Regan, Richard J: *Aquinas: The Cardinal Virtues*, 2005, Indianapolis, Hackett Publishing Co.

Stump, Eleonore: *Aquinas*, 2003, London, Routledge.

GLOSSARY

Aesthetics: The branch of philosophy which deals with art and beauty.

Androcentrism: The perception that maleness is normative in every facet of life; that all things are decided with reference only to the male point of view.

Anthropology: The study of humankind, including the whole constellation of cultural, philosophical and theological thought about what it means to be a human being. Feminist theologians consider anthropology, or the exploration of what it means to be human as female and male, to be one of their central concerns.

Appearance: Used in the appearance/reality distinction. How things seem to be, which may not be actually how they are.

Argument: A set of propositions which are structured as premises to a conclusion. The premises operate as reasons which lead to the conclusion. This abstract conception of an argument needs to be distinguished from the more normal conception of an argument as a heated debate between opponents. The former conception is the normal one in philosophy.

Assumption: Another word for a premise, or something which is assumed in an argument. It might be claimed to be obvious, or else is the conclusion of an earlier argument.

Augustine of Hippo (354-430 ce): Bishop of Hippo. Augustine, together with Thomas Aquinas, is considered to be among the main architects of Roman Catholic theology. His writing is foundational in every facet of the Christian life. His Confessions tell us more about his inner life than we know of most other ancient figures. From the perspective of feminist theology, however, Augustine is considered to have contributed definitively to the negative view of women, by his hesitation over whether or not women share the imago Dei.

Beatitude: Allows people to partake of the divine nature and of eternal life. With beatitude, people enter into the glory of Christ and into the joy of the Trinitarian life.

Belief: A mental state in which one holds something to be true. Note that a belief in this sense can be about anything, it is not restricted to being a religious notion.

Biblical prophetic tradition: Within the biblical tradition there is a continuous stream of persons appearing in times of community crisis to speak on behalf of God. Their message is always associated with the development of an alternative consciousness, that is, a way of looking at reality that is distinctly different from the dominant consciousness. The biblical prophets do this by speaking of reality from the perspective of the poor, the lowly, the excluded, the rejected, i.e. the perspective of those who are powerless in society. Much of feminist theology takes its biblical inspiration from this tradition.

Canon law: The code of ecclesiastical or Church law prescribed to Christians that came into force in 1918 ce. It is the set of rules or laws for the direction of the Christian faithful in matters of faith and conduct.

Cardinal virtues: The seven basic virtues upon which all other Christian virtues are considered to hinge: faith, hope, love, justice, prodence, temperance and fortitude.

Categories: The most general classifications, the basic kinds of features of things, for example quantity and quality.

Causation: A fundamental feature of the world is the pervasiveness of events causing other events. The analysis of causation is the attempt to explain the general features of this phenomenon; for example, are there causal powers in things, or is causation a projection from our minds?

Christian feminist movement: What is termed the second wave of the feminist movement (the first wave started from scriptural and secular beginnings in the nineteenth century), is associated with the movements for human rights in the sixties of the twentieth century. Together with the reforms of the Second Vatican Council, it challenged the Churches to attend to the reality of the presence, identity and ministry of women. There are now several Christian feminist movements, focusing, among other concerns, on theology, spirituality, ethics and ministry – especially the ordination of women. The central unifying principle is the affirmation of the full humanity of women.

Christology: This branch of theology focuses especially on the person and work of Jesus Christ, particularly as defined by the ecumenical councils of the early Church. The maleness of Jesus has focused the critique of feminist theologians and has led them to attempt a non-sexist interpretation of the significance of Jesus Christ.

Cognition: How beings acquire knowledge of themselves and their environment.

Conscience: According to Thomas Aquinas, conscience is the mind of the individual making moral judgements.

Conscientization: The process by which a person is changed from being a passive spectator to being someone who questions, and understands, things for her/himself.

Consciousness: The peculiar phenomenon of having a point of view, having a perspective, which is at the basis of subjectivity. There may be levels of consciousness and kinds of consciousness. It remains very hard to explain in objective terms.

Constantine (275-337 ce): The advent of the Emperor Constantine at the beginning of the fourth century made Christianity a legitimate religion of the Roman Empire. This signalled the end of persecution, but also tended to emphasise the imperialistic and universalising tendencies of Christianity.

Cosmogony: Theory about the origin of the universe.

Covenantal ethics: This term is used to signal a way of approaching ethical decisions that focuses on dialogue and reciprocal relationship, rooted in the biblical notion of the covenant of love between God and humanity, rather than on more authoritarian models of ethical thought and practice.

Critical awareness: An awareness that is informed by careful thought and reflection.

Decalogue: The Ten Commandments.

Deontological approach to morality: Duty-centred approach to morality, represented by Kant.

Dialectic: Another term for philosophical argumentation.

Dialectical method: Feminist theologians, in their challenge to male classical theology, tend to use a form of reasoning that includes the two components of critique and reconstruction. They critique forms of Christian thought which exclude the experience of women as a resource, and reconstruct theological thought rooted in the life, thought and experience of women.

Dilemma: An argument in which a position is shown to lead to two results, neither of which are acceptable. These results are known as the horns of the dilemma.

Divorce: Legal dissolution of a valid marriage.

Dualism: Dualistic thought understands the world in terms of a two-fold opposition, for example, male/female, heaven/earth, etc. The difficulty with such forms is that one side of the dualism is always seen as superior to the other. In this way, whole systems of thought can be built on an entirely negative image of the female. In philosophy of mind, the position that holds that mind and body are genuinely distinct substances.

Dualistic: The division of the world and human nature into matter and spirit.

Ecclesial: Relating to the Church.

Ecclesiological: Relating to the meaning of the Church in theology.

Ecofeminism: This relatively new term brings together the disciplines of ecology and feminism, especially in so far as the structures of domination which are central to both disciplines arise from the same source, namely the human domination of nature.

Economic Trinity: The exterior activity of God, in-so-far as it deals with the activity of the Triune God as manifested in the world and its history – as Father (Creator of the world), as Son (Redeemer of the world) and as Spirit (Reconciler of the world back to God).

Ecumenical feminist theology: The ecumenical movement of the twentieth century originated in the movement in many Churches toward cooperation on many fronts, especially in the area of work for justice and peace. Cooperation among feminist theologians on issues affecting women worldwide is now seen as an essential part of feminist theology.

Egoism: An excessive sense of one's own importance; conceit.

Eliminativism: In philosophy of mind, the position that holds that mind does not genuinely exist, it can be eliminated as a useful term and replaced with a scientific account of brain states.

Emergentism: In philosophy of mind, the position that holds that mind is a by-product of body, a function that emerges as bodies become more complex.

Enlightenment: Held that human reason possesses the power to find the truth about the human race, the world and God, and to live in accordance with this truth.

Epikeia: A term used by Thomas Aquinas to indicate fairness or good sense and should be used to recognise when human law might be inappropriate in a particular case. The application of Epikeia enhances justice, revealing glimpses of a higher 'law beyond the law'.

Epistemology: The part of philosophy which examines knowledge, its nature, kinds, sources and causes.

Eschatological: The dimension of theology that relates to the eschaton, or the ultimate destiny of things.

Essence: The feature of things which explains what kind of thing it is, what gives it its identity.

Ethics: The part of philosophy which examines practical reasoning, specifically about the good, justice, rights, duty, virtue and obligations.

Evil: That which is morally bad or harmful.

Existence: The feature of things which explains their instantiation, that they are actually there at all.

Existentialism: A school of philosophy whose origins are in the nineteenth century and which flourished in twentieth century continental Europe. It emphasised themes such as authenticity, meaninglessness, freedom of choice and absurdity. Associated with Kierkegaard, Nietzsche, Sartre, Heidegger, Marcel.

Externalism: An epistemological doctrine which holds that in order to know something, it is not necessary to know that you know, i.e. one can know something without being able to rationally defend one's claim to knowledge of that thing.

Faith: Belief in and commitment to something or someone. Christian faith is specifically a complete trust in Christ and his work as the basis of one's relationship to God.

Feminism: In the broadest sense this theory about women includes both a new way of looking at the world that is from the perspective of the experience of women, and also a new commitment to the flourishing of all women everywhere. It entails the development of a new vision and an alternative consciousness rooted in the interconnectedness of all created reality.

Feminist theology: Theology interprets scripture and tradition in specific theological and cultural contexts for the benefit of particular faith communities. Feminist theology focuses in particular on the place of and witness to women in scripture and tradition, and uses the experience of women as a central and essential resource for the doing of theology.

Fideism: A position in philosophy of religion which holds that reason cannot affect faith, they are two separate and non-connected realms. Faith may well contradict reason, but this is acceptable, as they are separate. Associated with Kierkegaard and Kant. It is a doctrine that religious truth is defined by faith and cannot be proved by reason.

Form: In Aristotle's metaphysics this refers to the structure which gives anything its identity. For Plato it refers to an abstract entity, beyond space and time, which is the reference of general terms, such as 'goodness'.

Formal logic: The branch of logic which systematises arguments and uses symbolism to do so.

Fortitude: One of the seven cardinal virtues: strength of mind which enables a person to bear adversity with courage.

Freedom, human: The concept that human beings freely determine their own bahaviour and that no external causal factors can adequately account for their actions.

Gnosticism: A movement in early Christianity, beginning already in the first century, which (1) emphasised a special higher truth that only the more enlightened receive from God, (2) taught that matter is evil, and (3) denied the humanity of Jesus.

Good, goodness: That which is morally excellent or, in the Christian framework. Accords with God's nature.

Grace: God's dealing with humankind in undeserved ways; it is simply an outflow of God's life, goodness and generosity.

Hedonism: A philosophy of life that perceives pleasure as the supreme good.

Hegemony: The domination of one person or culture or idea over all others.

Hellenistic: Adjective pertaining to later Greek philosophy, after the death of Aristotle (322 bce)

Hermeneutics: The science of interpretation and meaning.

Heteronomy: When moral duties are described literally as the will of God.

Historico-critical theology: The approach of theology which studies a text in the context of its earliest form, and how the meaning of that text is influenced – and transformed – by historical conditions down to the present.

Homoiousios: Proposed by Eusebius of Caesarea as the understanding of the Eastern Church – which means literally 'of a similar substance' or that the Son is 'like' the Father.

Homoousios: Used in the teaching of the early Church councils, especially Nicea (325 ce) to affirm that the Son is 'of one substance' ('consubstantial') with the Father, 'true God of true God' (Western or Latin influence).

Hope: The expectation of good things in the future; in the Christian tradition, faith regarding the matters that are yet to be.

Hypostasis: In Christian thought the term is used to refer to any one of the three distinct Persons in the Trinity, and especially Christ, the Second Person of the Trinity, in his divine and human natures.

Idealism: A metaphysical position which holds that mind is fundamental to the basic nature of reality. Opposed to realism, idealism comes in various forms. The kind covered in this module is 'subjective idealism', associated with the Irish philosopher, George Berkeley.

Identity: What something is, in its most general sense. Metaphysics seeks to articulate grounds for identity and to establish how identity relates to change, for example, what sorts of changes make something change its identity?

Ideology: Structure of beliefs which influences the behaviour of a group. Often used pejoratively to refer to set ways of thinking that justify vested interests or oppressive practices.

Imago Dei: A central element in the theological understanding of the human person is that each person is created in the image of God, imago Dei. Throughout the centuries many theologians, including Augustine of Hippo and Thomas Aquinas, questioned the application to women of this theological reality. This led to an understanding of women as being further removed from God than men were. The reclaiming of the imago Dei for women is a central plank in all feminist theologies.

Immanent Trinity: The hidden, unobservable, un-measurable, inner life of God as Trinity – in their differing relationships one to another; Father (un-begotten), Son (begotten), Spirit (proceeding from the Father and the Son).

Impasse: A situation of being unable to go either forward or back.

Inculturation: The insertion of a particular spirituality or 'way' into a foreign culture in a manner that respects that culture.

Ineffable: Beyond description, indescribable.

Inference: In logic, the moving from one proposition to another in a rational way.

Informal logic: The logic of ordinary language, contrasted with formal logic. Involves the presentation of forms of argument and how arguments go wrong, i.e. fallacies.

Innate: Usually associated with ideas. Ideas are innate if they are inborn, not coming from outside.

Intentionality: The feature of mental states (such as ideas) that they are 'about' something.

Internalism: An epistemological doctrine which holds that to know, one has to know that one knows. To know something genuinely means being able to rationally justify that knowledge. Opposed to externalism.

Interreligious: Links of communication between various religious traditions.

Intrinsic evil: Refers to actions that are so evil in themselves, that cannot ever be justified by motive or circumstance.

Judgment: Condemnation, or evaluation of one's guilt or innocence.

Justice: The principled operation of equality or fairness in a person and society. It covers issues such as the distribution of benefits and burdens (distributive justice) and how to deal with injustice (retributive justice).

Justification: In epistemology, justification is the process by which one gives reasons for holding a belief to be true.

Kingdom of God: Refers to the reign of God, the rule of God's grace in our hearts.

Kingdoms: Structures, political or social, of power and domination.

Knowledge: The object of epistemology; traditionally defined as 'justified true belief'.

Lectio divina: Reading the text of the Bible in a meditative and ruminative manner, acknowledging the place of the 'word' in the formation of everyday living.

Legalism: A point of view complemented by a corresponding emotional attitude which gives priority to a human structure rather than the Gospel purpose which it serves.

Liberationist agenda: The Gospel message of Jesus proclaimed liberty for captives and this has been seen as the core element in the proclamation of the Gospel in situations of social oppression. Feminist theology takes its stand within this liberating message.

Linguistic turn: A feature of twentieth century philosophy, where many of the traditional problems of philosophy are tackled by focussing on the use of language associated with them.

Logic: The science of inference – moving validly from one proposition to another with the goal of preserving truth. Formal logic is an abstract symbolic analysis of this process; informal logic is its use in normal discourse.

Love: One of the supreme attributes of God – concern for and action to bring about the welfare of another.

Magisterium: The teaching authority of the Catholic Church, derived from the medieval tradition of referring to the expert theologian as magister (master). Since the Reformation it has come to be restricted to collegial or papal teaching.

Manichaeism: A dualistic philosophy which became a major religion in the ancient world. There was a strong emphasis on upon asceticism as a means of salvation.

Marxist critique: This refers specifically to the Marxist socio-economic analysis of poverty and oppression. Liberation theology tends to keep this analysis separate from the ideological atheism and materialism of Marxism, though this separation is not valid according to many scholars.

Matter: In Aristotle's metaphysics, that which underlies form.

Metaphysics: The branch of philosophy which deals with the fundamental nature of reality. The study of substance, the essential nature of a thing.

Methodology: Feminist theologians draw attention to the fact that the way theology is done, the theological method, affects the content. This refers, in particular, to the interpretation of scripture, the understanding of tradition, the interpretation of experience and the questioning of whose experience counts, as well as the use of language and metaphor in the communication of theological truth. Feminist methodologies insist on self-critique, the inclusion of all voices, and the exploration of power structures that silence and marginalise some members of communities.

Monism (Monistic): Belief that reality consists of one basic substance, as opposed to being divided into physical and spiritual, good and evil, etc.

Monotheistic: Belief in one God.

Moral absolutes: Maintain their validity under any and every circumstance, no matter what.

Moral norms: Guides for ethical bahaviour.

Moral philosophy: The endeavour designed to determine which guides for action are worthy of acceptance and for what reasons.

Moral relativism: Gives people the freedom to create moral values and invent right and wrong.

Moral theology: The consideration of the principles which govern, or should govern, the behaviour of a Christian, and of their application in particular circumstances.

Morality: Conduct which is ethical.

Mortal sin: Sin which causes spiritual death. In Catholic theology, mortal sin extinguishes the life of God in the soul while venial sin merely weakens that life. With mortan sin there is a deliberate and intentional determination to resist God in everything one does, but with velial sin there is a tension between the wrongful action and the person committing it.

Natural law: When moral duties can be ascertained by reflection on human nature.

Natural theology: That part of metaphysics which discusses the issue of whether there is a God and what God's nature is, using pure reason and no religious resources.

Naturalism: As a metaphysical position this claims that there is nothing in existence which is not included in nature. As an epistemological position this claims that there is no kind of knowledge which does not fit into the natural sciences.

Neo-capitalism: The version of capitalism that is formed by the global market and that fosters the creation of consumer needs across the divides of world societies.

Neoplatonism: A school of Hellenistic philosophy which harmonised the work of Aristotle and Plato with the emphasis on Plato. Associated with Plotinus, Proclus, Augustine, Pseudo-Dionysius, Boethius.

Normative: Of or establishing a norm, standard, pattern, type.

Nominalism: The medieval doctrine that abstract concepts or universals do not have real existence but are simply names applied to qualities found within spercific individual objects.

Nous: The Greek word for mind. Used by Aristotle to also describe the faculty of grasping first principles of an argument, which themselves cannot be known on the basis of argument

Ontological: Dealing with the nature of being.

Pantheism: The view that God and nature are one.

Pantheon: A culture's collection of deities/gods.

Patriarchal Christianity: Patriarchy means literally the 'rule of the father' and is applied to Christianity in the traditional sense of exclusive male dominance in the leadership and teaching structures of almost all christian groups until fairly recently. Patriarchal Christianity continues to be the reality in the Roman Catholic tradition. The implication is, according to feminist theologians, that women have nothing of significance to offer in the areas of theology or teaching.

Patristic: Early Christian Fathers who had a major impact on the formation of the doctrinal tradition of the church.

Patristics: A branch of theology which deals with the work of the earliest Christian writers, known as the Fathers of the Church.

Pentecostalism: A movement which places great emphasis on the working of the Holy Spirit within the churches, and which is often very critical of other Christian traditions.

Philosophical theology: A branch of theology which uses philosophy to clarify and defend religious beliefs

Philosophy: The love of wisdom. An academic discipline which addresses fundamental questions about the nature of reality, knowledge, mind and value, not addressed by specific disciplines such as physics or psychology.

Phronesis: Practical reasoning. The kind of knowledge used in making moral judgements.

Praxis: From the Greek, meaning practical action, and used by liberation theology to denote a combination of action and reflection aimed at transforming an oppressive situation.

Premise: An assumption used in argumentation. A valid argument is one whose premises, if true, require that the conclusion also be true.

Presocratic: Referring to the philosophy which came before Socrates.

Proportionalism: The doctrine which suggests that a judgement whether any action is good or evil can be determined by weighing the positive results of the action against its negative results.

Proposition: The philosophical term used for a sentence. It concerns the cognitive content of the sentence, rather than style or language. The following three sentences express the same proposition: "It is raining", "Il pleut", "Ta se ag cur baisteach".

Protagonists: The main participants in an event or a story.

Prudence: Careful, judicious action, or the wisdom that lies behind such action.

Realism: The metaphysical position which holds that reality exists independently of mind.

Reason: The power of thinking, comprehending and inferring.

Reductionism: In philosophy, this is the claim that some area under discussion is best understood by reference to another area. For example, someone might claim that mental talk is best explained by reference to brain function, that all talk of ideas and thoughts is best understood by reducing it to physical operations in the head. The advantage of reductionism is clarity, the disadvantage is the fear of leaving aside what is important.

Relativism: The claim that no single view of things is the correct one, but that there is a multiplicity of alternative, equally correct, views of e.g. reality, knowledge, truth, values.

Representationalism: A view in epistemology which holds that we do not have direct access to reality, but rather know it by means of representations, or ideas, which mediate the world to us.

Revelation: The maing known of that which is unknown.

Scholasticism: A term used to describe later medieval philosophy which makes extensive use of Aristotle's philosophy.

Second Vatican Council: The twenty-first ecumenical (i.e. universal) council in the history of the church, and the greatest in its number of bishops participating and of documents produced. Pope John XXIII convened it, and it was closed by Pope Paul VI. It was held in the church of St Peter, in the Vatican City, and met in four sessions (October-December 1962; September-December 1963; September-November 1964; and September-December 1965).

Seminal: Influential in future development, from the Latin semen, meaning seed.

Sexual asceticism: The monastic phenomenon which took root in Christianity in the late third century was based on the renunciation of the world, and especially of the human sexual dimension. A significant strand of christian tradition saw the renunciation of sexuality as the most important element of the christian faith. This led to little attention being paid to the spiritual richness of marriage and this continues to affect christian spirituality to our own day,

Sin: According to St Augustine sin is any word or deed or thought against the eternal law.

Skepticism: In general, this is a philosophical position which denies that we have any speculative knowledge of things beyond ordinary beliefs (for example metaphysics or theology). It comes in many kinds.

Social analysis: The study of factors that form a particular social structure or phenomenon (e.g. a family, or the reality of migration), and their relationship with one another.

Sophia: The Greek word for wisdom, knowledge of the highest things.

Sophist: Teacher of rhetoric in ancient athens. Used as a pejorative term of one who is more interested in literary style than in truth.

Soul: The English word for the Greek word psyche and the Latin word anima. It is the principle which makes living things living. Some philosophers claim that the human soul, capable of reasoning is immortal. Others deny that it makes sense to think of the soul as a substance, rather it is a function of the body and dies with it.

Substance: A major area of investigation for metaphysics, with many competing accounts. Philosophers speak of substance as the most fundamental kind of existing thing, distinguishing it from property.

Subversive: Refers to the overthrow or the corruption of something.

Syllogism: A form of argument, in which two premises lead to a conclusion, for example "All humans are mortal, Socrates is human, Socrates is mortal". There are strict rules governing validity for syllogisms.

Temperance: Moderation in everything.

Teleology: A teleological approach to morality, focusing exclusively on the consequences of acts.

Term: The basic meaningful unit in a proposition under logical analysis. The proposition 'Socrates is Greek' consists of three terms; subject (the object under consideration) Socrates, predicate (the property attributed to the subject) Greek, and copula (the manner in which the predicate is connected to the subject, in this case affirmatively) is.

Theism: The claim that there exists a god who is an eternal, perfect creator.

Theodicy: Part of philosophy of religion which attempts to show the compatibility of the existence of God with the prevalence of evil.

Theological virtues: These are infused by God into the souls of the faithful to enable us to act as children of God and to merit eternal life.

Theology: A general term for the kind of reasoning which uses data from revealed religion.

Truth: A property of a proposition or a belief in which what it states to be the case actually is the case.

Universal: An abstract entity which is the meaning of a general term, such as 'goodness'. The problem of universals is the debate as to whether any such universals exist in reality.

Utilitarianism: An ethical theory which evaluiates acts by their consequences and particularly by the criterion of the greatest good for the greatest number.

Utopian: Refers to an imaginary and ideal place, and associated with Thomas Moreís political work, Utopia (1516).

Validity: A property of arguments. A valid argument is one whose structure is such that if the premises are true, then the conclusion has to be also true.

Virtue: An excellence of character or mind which is a fine balance between two opposing vices, for example, courage is opposed to both cowardice and foolhardiness; Recurrent and unwavering disposition to do the good.

THEOLOGY FOR TODAY
FUNDAMENTAL MORAL THEOLOGY
VOLUME ONE

UNIT ONE:
FUNDAMENTAL MORAL CONCEPTS

UNIT TWO:
NATURE, REASON, LAW AND GROWTH

From time immemorial the human race has asked questions about right and wrong. Opinions differ, not only in particular instances but also on the very notion of what constitutes right and wrong.

Unit One of this module – Fundamental Moral Theology – begins by asking: 'Why be moral'? Different schools of thought have produced differing answers to this question, the most important of which are outlined in this unit.

The module then examines all the elements involved when a person performs a morally responsible action – what is called 'a human act'. Throughout this module, it will be clear that in Catholic moral thinking the use of reason is paramount in determining the goodness of moral actions.

THE
PRIORY
INSTITUTE

Tallaght Village, Dublin 24, Ireland
Tel: 01 4048124. Fax: 01 404 6084
Email: enquiries@prioryinstitute.com

ISBN 1-905193-16-5

9 781905 193165

THE
PRIORY
INSTITUTE

THEOLOGY FOR TODAY

FUNDAMENTAL MORAL THEOLOGY
VOLUME TWO